The Right to Die

by Anne Wallace Sharp

LUCENT BOOKS
A part of Gale, Cengage Learning

GALE
CENGAGE Learning™

Detroit • New York • San Francisco • New Haven, Conn • Waterville, Maine • London

GALE
CENGAGE Learning™

LIBRARY OF CONGRESS CATALOGING-IN-PUBLICATION DATA

Sharp, Anne Wallace.
  The right to die / By Anne Wallace Sharp.
    p. cm. — (Hot topics)
  Includes bibliographical references and index.
  ISBN 978-1-59018-834-7 (hardcover)
    1. Right to die—Law and legislation—United States—Juvenile literature.
  2. Euthanasia—Law and legislation—United States—Juvenile literature.
  I. Title.
    KF3827.E87S5 2009
    344.7304'197—dc22

                                                    2008037029

Lucent Books
27500 Drake Rd.
Farmington Hills, MI 48331

ISBN-13: 978-1-59018-834-7
ISBN-10: 1-59018-834-9

Printed in the United States of America
2 3 4 5 6 7 13 12 11 10 09

CONTENTS

FOREWORD

Young people today are bombarded with information. Aside from traditional sources such as newspapers, television, and the radio, they are inundated with a nearly continuous stream of data from electronic media. They send and receive e-mails and instant messages, read and write online "blogs," participate in chat rooms and forums, and surf the Web for hours. This trend is likely to continue. As Patricia Senn Breivik, the former dean of university libraries at Wayne State University in Detroit, has stated, "Information overload will only increase in the future. By 2020, for example, the available body of information is expected to double every 73 days! How will these students find the information they need in this coming tidal wave of information?"

Ironically, this overabundance of information can actually impede efforts to understand complex issues. Whether the topic is abortion, the death penalty, gay rights, or obesity, the deluge of fact and opinion that floods the print and electronic media is overwhelming. The news media report the results of polls and studies that contradict one another. Cable news shows, talk radio programs, and newspaper editorials promote narrow viewpoints and omit facts that challenge their own political biases. The World Wide Web is an electronic minefield where legitimate scholars compete with the postings of ordinary citizens who may or may not be well informed or capable of reasoned argument. At times, strongly worded testimonials and opinion pieces both in print and electronic media are presented as factual accounts.

Conflicting quotes and statistics can confuse even the most diligent researchers. A good example of this is the question of whether or not the death penalty deters crime. For instance, one study found that murders decreased by nearly one-third when the death penalty was reinstated in New York in 1995. Death penalty supporters cite this finding to support their argument that the existence of the death penalty deters criminals from committing murder. However, another study found that states without the death penalty have murder rates below the national average. This study is cited by opponents of capital punishment, who reject the claim that the death penalty deters murder. Students need context and clear, informed discussion if they are to think critically and make informed decisions.

The Hot Topics series is designed to help young people wade through the glut of fact, opinion, and rhetoric so that they can think critically about controversial issues. Only by reading and thinking critically will they be able to formulate a viewpoint that is not simply the parroted views of others. Each volume of the series focuses on one of today's most pressing social issues and provides a balanced overview of the topic. Carefully crafted narrative, fully documented primary and secondary source quotes, informative sidebars, and study questions all provide excellent starting points for research and discussion. Full-color photographs and charts enhance all volumes in the series. With its many useful features, the Hot Topics series is a valuable resource for young people struggling to understand the pressing issues of the modern era.

INTRODUCTION

THE RIGHT
TO DIE

Death is one of the most emotionally charged times in any individual's life. Human beings have struggled since ancient times to understand and deal with the dying process. Death has always been greatly feared, but it can also be viewed as being just another stage of life.

The concept of the right to die, however, is a modern concept and a modern issue. The term came into existence in the latter half of the twentieth century as a result of advancements made in medical technology. With the advent of cardiopulmonary resuscitation and the invention of artificial respirators and other machines, an individual's life could be prolonged and sustained even in the direst of circumstances.

There is no single definition of the phrase "right to die," for it means many different things to different people. For a person suffering from a fatal or terminal disease, it might mean stopping aggressive treatment such as chemotherapy and dying in a natural way. For others with the same fatal illness, the right to die might include the right to petition a physician for a fatal dose of medication.

For yet other individuals, the right to die involves other decisions. For certain religious groups who believe in prayer for curing illness, the decision might involve refusing to seek traditional medical care or have a blood transfusion. For a person who has been totally paralyzed from some kind of severe accident, it might denote asking the physician to remove a ventilator that is the only thing keeping him or her alive. The same decision becomes more complicated when the individual is not in a position to make his or her own decisions because of an irreversible coma or sleeplike trance. Then the choice must be made by a family member: Should life-sustaining treatment continue, or should it be stopped?

All of these decisions are difficult because they involve life and death choices. Those individuals who support the concept of the right to die argue that such decisions should be an individual's choice. For such supporters the issue can be easily stated: People should have the right to end their lives at a time and in a manner of their own choosing. Author George M. Burnell elaborates, "Dying should be a matter of personal choice."[1]

Those who oppose an individual's right to die contend that the issue is far more complicated. First of all, they argue that the act of a physician giving a patient a fatal dose of medicine is illegal

As the American population ages, the number of people needing medical care will put a strain on health care resources.

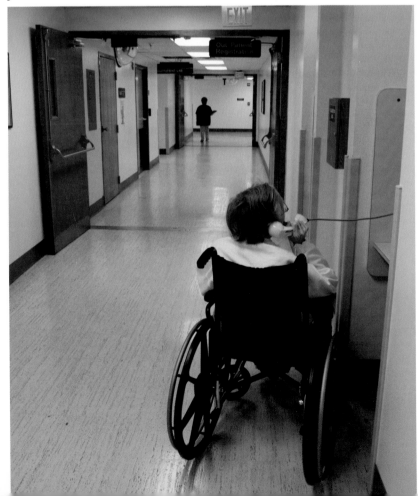

in the United States, with the exception of the state of Oregon. Secondly, they assert that ending the life of a loved one, whether by direct intervention or by the removal of life-sustaining treatment, constitutes murder or manslaughter. Lastly, right-to-life supporters argue that all life is sacred, a gift from God, and that only God can end a life. The Episcopal Church speaks for many religions when it says, "It is morally wrong and unacceptable to intentionally take a human life."[2]

The issues surrounding end-of-life decisions are complicated by an aging population. The average life expectancy in 1900 was forty-one years of age; by the year 2000, the age had increased to seventy-seven. With people living longer and also having more chronic illnesses, the medical profession faces new issues. Journalist Ted Gest, writing in 1989, examined this question: "As health care resources grow scarce in the next fifty years, the population over sixty-five will multiply three times . . . raising wrenching questions about who deserves treatment."[3]

Most Americans are living longer. This makes the right to die an important issue that must be resolved. Even medicine has limited resources, as author and right-to-die supporter Donald W. Cox explains: "The increasingly high costs of keeping incurable patients alive are bringing greater pressures on legislators to do something to meet this daunting burden."[4] With an increased life span and a new emphasis on the quality of life, rather than the quantity, almost everyone agrees that important decisions must be made to ensure and achieve that quality.

Many of the questions surrounding the right-to-die issue remain unanswered today. While various courts have ruled on cases involving a person's right to die, the results have been confusing. Some courts have upheld a person's right to make such decisions, while others have denied that right. State legislatures have also failed to define clearly an individual's rights in end-of-life decisions.

Cox, former president of the Hemlock Society of Delaware Valley, a right-to-die group, states, "Individuals should have the right to die with dignity at the time and manner of their choice, but they also have a right to live."[5] Seeking a balance between these two extremes is an ethical problem that continues to be debated by physicians, politicians, ethicists, and others.

DEATH AND THE DYING PROCESS

Few people want to talk or even think about death and dying. For most, just the thought of one's own death causes great fear. Swiss physician and the author of the book *On Death and Dying* Elisabeth Kübler-Ross elaborates, "Death is still a fearful, frightening happening and the fear of death is a universal fear."[6] Death reminds of us our vulnerability and our own mortality.

Most people, when they do think about death, believe it is something that is far removed, distant, and nearly inconceivable. Death is something that happens to other people, not to them. However, "dying is one of the few events in life certain to occur," elaborates *Time* journalist John Cloud, "and yet one we are not likely to plan for. We will spend more time getting ready for two weeks away from work than we will for our last two weeks on earth."[7]

For many people, dying may involve the loss of faith, the loss of hope, and often a feeling of being abandoned by God. For those who believe in an afterlife or a heaven, however, death is also viewed as a transition from one state of human existence to another. Just as each individual has his or her own way of living, it is now believed that each also has his or her own way of dying.

Whatever one believes, however, death has always fascinated people. It has also been clouded by myth and by the portrayal of death in the media. Death has been depicted throughout history in images that range from merely going to sleep to a brutal and painful end. These various presentations, rather than calming fears, have served to further confuse and alarm people. Thus, author Burnell concludes, "To make death no longer a source of dread is one of the great challenges of the age."[8]

Early Beliefs About Death and Dying

From the beginning of history, people have viewed death as inevitable and universal. Yet different cultures have reacted to death and dying in different ways. These viewpoints have been affected by religious beliefs, cultural traditions, and the availability of medical resources.

The early Romans and Greeks, for instance, greatly feared death. This fear is evident in their myths and their beliefs in many gods and goddesses who exacted punishment on humans for various sins. In many instances these gods were vengeful and caused great suffering among the human race.

During the Middle Ages, many people believed that suffering was always part of the dying process and, therefore, had to be borne silently and stoically. Many Christians believed that this

The topic of death has always troubled people.

The ancient Greeks showed their fear of death in their art and literature, in which they depicted humans suffering punishment at the hands of vengeful gods. This Greek statue shows the character of Laocoön and his two sons being strangled by sea serpents after angering the gods.

prolonged suffering actually gave the dying a chance to put their affairs in order and make amends to people and the church for their various sins.

Most of the early indigenous people of North America, South America, Asia, Australia, and Europe did not fear death; they considered death a part of life. They believed that death was not the end of life but rather a part of nature's never-ending cycle. They also believed in an afterlife where a person lived in peace and harmony much as they had done during their years on earth. As a result, many older people chose death rather than burdening their community with their aging needs such as daily care and feeding.

In certain Inuit (formerly called Eskimo) cultures, for instance, old or sick individuals were allowed to petition for death by simply telling their families that they were ready to die. These older people preferred to stay or be left behind on the ice to die naturally rather than burdening their family and tribe with their aging needs. Historians James M. Hoefler and Brian E. Kamore elaborate, "Eskimos believe that anyone dying in this way spends eternity in the highest of heavens."[9]

DYING IS A STAGE OF GROWTH

"Much of our society's crisis around death could be said to stem from a lack of awareness of the dying process as a stage of growth. Just as different steps must be mastered from childhood, adolescence, and adulthood, dying presents its own challenges." —Journalist Pythia Peay.

Pythia Peay, "A Good Death," *Common Boundary*, September/October 1997, p. 34.

Elderly and ill Blackfoot of Canada and the Northern Plains also acted in this manner. When older people felt life coming to an end, they often disposed of all their property and belongings and then willingly left the village to find a quiet spot to die. Occasionally, in times of hardship or starvation, the elderly were simply abandoned by the tribe. There was no guilt or condemnation attached to this practice, and the people involved willingly stayed behind to lessen the impact on the remainder of the community.

A Good Death

These indigenous cultures would have described such deaths as "good ones." Not only did the elderly elect to die in a manner of their own choosing, but their deaths were viewed by the entire community as both natural and meaningful. In modern society, most people yearn for a similar "good death." Journalist Richard Venus elaborates, "A good death is one in which we are at peace, without a great loss of dignity, without so much pain that it becomes our sole focus; a death that does not add terrible anguish to those who love and care for us."[10]

Nineteenth-century hospitals, as shown in this drawing, were generally dirty places that served as breeding grounds for infection.

A good death, according to most public opinion polls, is a natural death, which excludes suicide or homicide. It is relatively painless, with a person dying surrounded and supported by his or her loved ones. It also involves a person who has accepted death and is ready to die, made possible by saying goodbye to loved ones and making amends for any wrongdoing. Finally, a good death is one that happens at home.

Home deaths were common until the last half of the twentieth century. During the nineteenth century, for instance, hospitals were few and provided only basic food, shelter, and minimum nursing care to patients. Surgery was very primitive and primarily involved the amputation of limbs and a few other simple procedures. Few really sound medical treatments were available for the sick. For the most part, hospitals were run by religious and charity groups.

These early hospitals were often dangerous places to be. Doctors knew very little about the importance of sanitary conditions and, as a result, infections spread rapidly in the hospital setting. Even basic cleanliness techniques were slow in developing. Hospitals, as a rule, were dirty, smelly places to be avoided. Thus, most people stayed home when they were ill and when they were dying.

A Move Toward Hospital Care

Hospitals began improving toward the beginning of the twentieth century as more and more were built. In 1872, for instance, the United States had less than two hundred hospitals countrywide. By 1910 there were over four thousand. The discovery of radiation and the use of X-ray technology, better infection control, improvements in surgery, and better pain medications helped lead to this boom in hospitals. More and more people began relying on hospital care for major illnesses and surgeries.

The 1960s saw the birth of specialization among physicians. Family doctors, while still taking care of a patient's basic needs, gave way to specialists in every imaginable field. A hospitalized patient in critical condition, for instance, might end up having a dozen different physicians caring for him or her. Patients benefited from this expertise by having specialized doctors dealing with specific problems, but they also suffered. They began to feel that their doctors had less of a personal interest in them. Patients also felt bombarded with various medical opinions. And in most cases, they felt left out of the decision-making process.

Despite people still wanting to die at home, more and more deaths began to occur in hospital settings. In fact, as of the beginning of the twenty-first century, nearly half of all Americans die not only in hospitals, but in pain, surrounded and treated by strangers, and separated from their families. John Farrell, chair of surgery at the University of Miami in the 1950s, explains:

> In our pursuit of the scientific aspects of science, the art of medicine has sometimes unwittingly and justifiably suffered. . . . The death bed scenes I witness are not particularly dignified. The family is shoved out into the cor-

Bioethics

Beginning in the late 1960s, because of increased public awareness of people's rights as patients, physicians and hospitals often found their decisions being questioned and challenged. This, as well as the technological advances in medicine and a new definition of death, brought about the creation of bioethics committees in all the major hospitals. Ethics has been defined as the study of principles; bioethics became the study of moral principles as they related to medicine.

Hospitals used bioethics committees to decide all major ethical decisions. These included decisions relating to the welfare of the patient, the withdrawal of life-sustaining treatment, and the settlement of disputes between patients and their physicians. The committees are also charged with educating hospital staff on ethical questions such as the ones listed above. Today when a conflict arises between a doctor and patient on the course of treatment, the problem is referred to the hospital ethics committee.

ridor by the physical presence of intravenous stands, suction machines, oxygen tanks, and tubes emanating from every natural and several surgically induced orifices. The last words . . . are lost behind an oxygen mask.[11]

In addition, death, once viewed as a natural part of life, has come to be seen as a failure by doctors and hospitals alike. Death has become an unacceptable outcome and often an embarrassment for modern medical practitioners. Hospitals may be the best place to receive advanced treatment for acute diseases, but many are ill-prepared to help or allow patients to die. "The modern hospital is the greatest enemy of meaningful death,"[12] wrote John Carmody, a former priest, about his own father's death in a hospital.

Charles F. McKhann, a specialist in cancer surgery, agrees. His interest in the subject grew out of his father's death from cancer in a hospital. His father was kept alive for nearly three months, even though his outlook was totally hopeless. Treatment included intravenous fluids, blood transfusions, and other aggressive measures. McKhann wrote: "An intelligent, competent

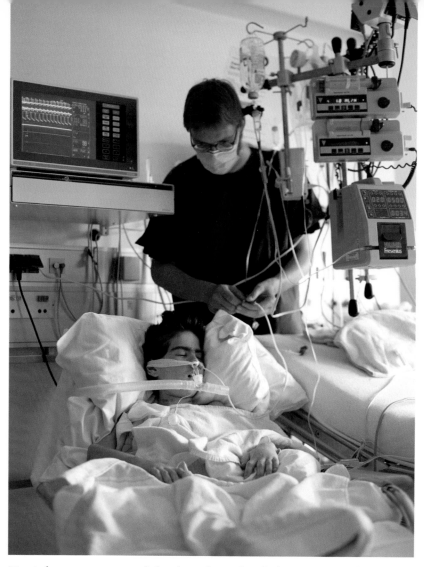

Hospital rooms are so crowded with machines that the human aspect of medicine is often lost.

man, himself a physician, hospitalized in a major medical center, had absolutely no control over stopping useless treatment. . . . It seems unfair that people who manage their own affairs successfully in life should be required to turn over so much of their death and dying to others."[13]

McKhann's experience has been shared by countless others. In the late twentieth century, for instance, it was estimated that Americans spent an average of eighty days in the hospital during the year they died. Americans are also spending more time in nursing homes and similar facilities.

Defining Death

Whether dying took place in a hospital or at home, for many decades death simply meant the cessation of breathing and heart function. With the advent of resuscitation methods and mechanical ventilators, knowing when death occurred became more difficult. These medical technologies could keep an unconscious person alive for an indefinite amount of time. The line between life and death began to blur.

The first major development that changed how people viewed death was the use of cardiopulmonary resuscitation. Physicians realized that if emergency breathing and other techniques were performed in the first few minutes after a patient collapsed from a cardiac arrest (usually caused by a heart attack), that patient had a good chance of recovering. Rescue breathing and artificial pumping of the heart could keep an individual alive until he or she reached the hospital, where more advanced techniques could improve the person's chance of surviving.

A TIME OF OPPORTUNITY

"The experience of dying can . . . be understood as a part of full and healthy living, as a time of caring and as a time of remarkable opportunity for persons, families, and communities." —Hospice physician Ira R. Byock.

Quoted in Robert F. Weir, *Physician-Assisted Suicide*. Bloomington: Indiana University Press, 1997, p. 132.

Then came the development of even more advanced ways to resuscitate a patient. Bernard Lown was one of the first physicians to use electric shock to restart a patient's heart in the early 1960s. He began to investigate the use of electrical currents and invented a primitive defibrillator, a machine that delivered electric shock to the body in the hopes of restarting the heart and correcting fatal heart rhythms. He also helped develop one of the United States' first coronary intensive care units. By the mid-1960s mobile "crash carts" for use in cardiac arrest were common in intensive care units and hospitals throughout the country. Many patients who previously would have died were given a new chance at life with the use of these machines and techniques.

In addition to the use of resuscitation techniques and a defibrillator, several other devices were invented and refined that enabled patients to survive normally fatal occurrences. A massive machine called an iron lung was developed in the 1950s for polio patients who needed assistance in breathing. This machine was unwieldy in size and configuration, but it enabled paralyzed patients to continue breathing. This led to the development of

The use of cardiopulmonary resuscitation (CPR), demonstrated in this picture by two firefighters on a CPR dummy, changed the way people viewed death.

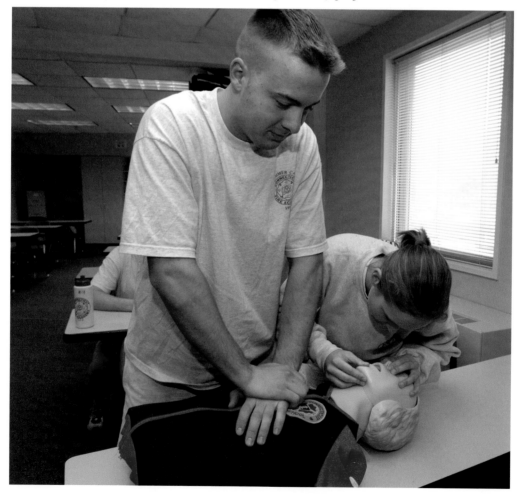

bedside ventilators that were able to breathe for the patient. The ventilator enabled patients who were in a coma to survive for longer periods of time, especially when the patient was unable to breathe on his or her own. Prior to this invention, many patients who were comatose or severely injured died as a result of respiratory arrest or the inability to breathe on their own. Writers Hoefler and Kamore summarize, "Advances in both diagnostic and rescue-medicine technology have helped to create a whole population of individuals who would have died quickly only a few decades ago."[14]

In addition to the development of resuscitation techniques, other medical advances led to new treatments that also prolonged life. Patients with life-threatening kidney failure, for instance, were able to live longer through the use of dialysis, a technique that removed toxins from a patient's body by recycling the blood through filters. Advances in the treatment of diabetes, asthma, and infectious diseases through the development of drugs enabled longer survival rates with those illnesses. Finally, improved surgical techniques and care of pregnant women and their newborns decreased the death rate in those areas of medicine. While all of these treatments prolonged life and improved mortality rates, they did not affect the definition of death. Since a person's death could be postponed indefinitely by these new technological advances that could keep a patient's heart and respiratory system functioning, the old definition of death needed revising.

A New Definition—Brain Death

The need for a new definition of death became critical on December 3, 1967, with the first successful heart transplant operation by Christiaan Barnard in South Africa. For the first time, a severely diseased heart was removed and replaced with a healthy heart from a recently deceased person. As transplant surgery became more successful and more popular, the question arose as to when a dying person's organs could be harvested or removed for transplant. It was necessary to harvest organs in a timely fashion following death; in fact, mere seconds could make the difference between a viable organ and one that could not be used. Doctors realized that if someone was being kept alive artificially despite all other signs of death, with the family's permission, organs could be removed at the exact moment of death, thus preserving healthy organs. Medicine and society needed to come up with a new definition of death to enable perfectly good organs in a dying patient to be used to help heal another one. Journalist Pythia Peay contends that with transplantation came a blurring of the definition of death: "As medicine has advanced to extend life despite grave illness, the boundaries between a natural death and an artificially sustained life have become blurred."[15]

The new life-sustaining technologies made the traditional boundary between life and death murky. In order to clarify this boundary and to make more transplantations successful, the medical community moved toward formulating a new definition of death. The task of creating this definition fell to the Harvard Brain Death Committee, a group of physicians and ethicists who met and later published their conclusions in the *Journal of the American Medical Association* (*JAMA*).

GRANTING CONTROL TO THE DYING

"Findings suggest that dying patients should be allowed as much control over their lives and routines, and life should, as far as possible, be consistent with the life they led before their illness; this applies especially in their relationships with important people in their lives and being allowed to spend as much time as possible in familiar and comfortable surroundings." —Writers Joseph Braga and Laurie Braga.

Joseph Braga and Laurie Braga, *Death: The Final Stage of Growth.* Englewood Cliffs, NJ: Prentice Hall, 1975, p. 75.

In 1968, after extensive consultation, the committee issued its report: "Our primary purpose is to define irreversible coma as a new criterion for death." Speaking for the committee, Henry Beecher elaborated that, in addition, their purpose was "to choose a level where, although the brain is dead, usefulness of other organs is still present."[16] Journalists Edd Doerr and M.L. Tina Stevens further explain that the committee wanted to construct "guidelines that left as little room as possible for a legal charge

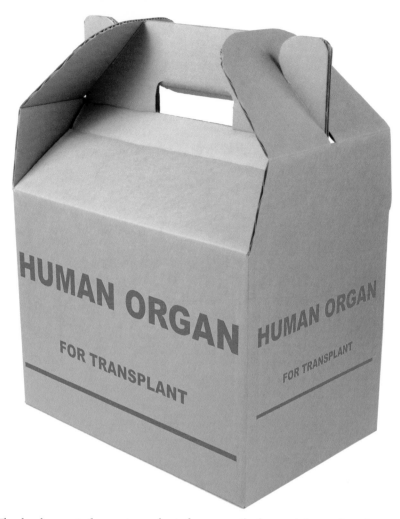

The development of organ transplants from recently deceased donors forced medicine to come up with a new definition of death.

that they were removing organs from people who have even a modest chance of recovery."[17]

The Harvard committee listed a number of symptoms or conditions that had to be present in order to classify a death as "brain death." The primary criterion was a flat electroencephalogram (EEG), an electrical recording of brain waves and brain activity. A flat EEG meant that the brain was essentially nonfunctioning or dead. In addition, the patient had to be nonresponsive to any stimuli, including pain, and also lack any voluntary movement. Finally, brain death was apparent when the patient had no involuntary reflexes and the pupils of the eye were dilated and fixed or nonresponsive to light.

The new definition was particularly useful for patients who were diagnosed as being in an irreversible coma. In the past such patients had not been considered dead under the old guidelines, because their breathing and heart continued to function. With the new criteria, life support could theoretically be stopped for patients who met the brain death criteria.

THE FEAR

"There is a deep-seated fear of high-tech medicine in America, of being locked into machines and losing control of their own lives." —Hemlock Society founder Derek Humphry.

Quoted in Donald W. Cox, *Hemlock's Cup: The Struggle for Death with Dignity*. Buffalo, NY: Prometheus, 1993, p. 27.

Between 1970 and 1981, twenty-seven different states adopted legislation that allowed physicians to use the brain death criteria. The laws also permitted doctors to end life support without fear of prosecution in such cases. Since the 1980s the remaining states have similarly used the definition of brain death.

The Death Awareness Movement

Around the same time that the Harvard committee was issuing its new definition, another notable event occurred that directly impacted the perception of death by both the medical profession and the public. That event was the publication of Swiss physician Elisabeth Kübler-Ross's best-selling book *On Death and Dying* in 1969.

Born in Zurich, Switzerland, Kübler-Ross began her work with the terminally ill at the University of Colorado. She later became a clinical professor of behavioral medicine and psychiatry at the University of Virginia. Kübler-Ross focused her studies on the terminally ill and discovered that contrary to medical thought, these patients were eager to talk about their experiences.

Her interviews with the dying led her to put her thoughts into book form. Kübler-Ross called for "the rejection of a lonely, mechanical, dehumanized environment for the dying."[18] She concluded that the dying were often isolated in sterile hospital environ-

Elisabeth Kübler-Ross's book On Death and Dying *(1969) is credited with starting the "death awareness" movement.*

ments, separated by technology from their loved ones, and often left to suffer in pain prior to their deaths. In addition, she found that few physicians actually consulted their terminal patients on their course of treatment. She wrote, "Dying nowadays is more gruesome in many ways, namely, more lonely, mechanical, and dehumanized."[19] She suggested that because so many people feared and ignored death, the dying were also often feared and ignored.

The publication of this book is often credited with the birth of the "death awareness" movement. As a result of her book, increasing numbers of physicians, nurses, psychologists, and social workers began to study the concepts of death and dying, and in particular the care of the terminally ill. According to Stephen Connor, vice president of the National Hospice and Palliative Care Organization, Kübler-Ross "brought the taboo notion of death and dying into the public consciousness."[20]

Stages of Grief

Elisabeth Kübler-Ross revolutionized the way the public looked at the dying process. From her interviews with the terminally ill, she identified five stages that all dying people progress through. The first stage is denial. Most patients react in shock when they receive a diagnosis of a terminal disease, often saying, "No, not me, it can't be true." Then comes the stage of anger. This anger is directed at the disease, at the doctors who diagnosed it, and often at God. Why me? is a question often asked by people in this stage of the grief process.

Anger is followed by bargaining. Many patients silently try to bargain with God, promising to do this or that if only the diagnosis could change. This usually brief phase is followed by depression as the truth of the matter settles in. Patients often feel a sense of hopelessness. They feel burdened with financial concerns and other unfinished business. In many cases depression deepens as the fatal disease causes more and more weakness and loss of function.

The final stage is acceptance. For many, acceptance comes late in the disease process, often in the days leading up to death. M. Christina Puchalski writes, "The dying need an opportunity to bring closure to their lives by forgiving those they had conflicts with, making peace with themselves and God, and saying goodbye to friends and family." Even at this stage, many patients still hope for a miracle in the form of a new drug or a new treatment. They are trying to maintain a small thread of hope that will keep them going through the worst of the disease.

Quoted in James Haley, ed., *Death and Dying: Opposing Viewpoints*. Farmington Hills, MI: Greenhaven, 2003, p. 73.

Death as a Public Issue

Partially as a result of Kübler-Ross's work, in the late 1960s and early 1970s, death began to be widely discussed not only by the medical profession, but by the general public. There was an abundance of television shows, books, and movies about death and the dying process. From 1968 to 1973, for instance, the number of articles about death in mainstream American magazines doubled and then redoubled. Over twelve hundred new books on death and dying were published during that same five-year period. In addition, people flocked to weekend seminars focusing on these issues. Americans became nearly obsessed with death and dying.

This obsession arose as a result of several social factors in addition to Kübler-Ross's work. The 1960s, for instance, was a period of great unrest in the United States as the civil rights movement impacted the lives of Americans throughout the country. As blacks fought to gain equal rights, the consciousnesses of many Americans were awakened to the injustices that occurred in daily life. This led to a reexamination of individual rights in America and spawned the women's rights movement. With an emphasis on individual rights, there was also a phenomenal growth of self-help groups and the use of psychotherapy. From there it was a natural outgrowth to an increased interest in each person's right to

The American Hospital Association adopted the Patient's Bill of Rights in 1973, part of which allows patients and their families to decline extraordinary medical treatments.

A PATIENT'S BILL OF RIGHTS *Skin & Laser Center*

The office of <u>GREATER MIAMI SKIN AND LASER CENTER</u> presents a Patient's Bill of Rights with the expectation that observance of these rights will contribute to more effective patient care and greater satisfaction for the patient, his physician and the group organization. It is recognized as proper medical care. The traditional physician-patient relationship takes on a new dimension when care is rendered within an organizational structure. Legal precedent has established that the facility it self also has a responsibility to the patient. It is in recognition of these factors that rights are affirmed.

<u>The patient has the right:</u>

1. To respectful treatment with concern for individual, cultural or education difference.

2. To complete, up to date information about the condition, treatment and outlook for recovery.

3. To know who is responsible for the care provided.

4. To personal privacy and confidentiality in communication and medical records.

5. To refuse treatment, except in some cases where life saving treatment is mandated.

6. To know of any affiliations your hospital and physician(s) have with other institutions and physicians.

<u>The patient has the responsibility:</u>

1. To provide accurate and complete information about present complaints, past illnesses, hospitalizations, medications and other health related matters.

2. To report any unexpected change in condition to the responsible physician.

3. To say whether a contemplated course of treatment and the patient's obligation in its administration are understood.

4. To follow the treatment plan recommended by the physician. The patient is expected to follow up on his/her doctor's instructions, take medication when prescribed, and ask questions concerning his/her own health care that he/she feels is necessary.

5. To keep appointments or notify the appropriate person if it is not possible to do so.

6. To accept the consequences of choosing to ignore physician instructions or to refuse treatment ...obligations assumed in receiving health care are met as promptly as

READ IF YOU ARE USING YOUR INSURANCE CARD

IT IS OUR OFFICE POLICY TO REQUEST A COPY OF YOUR DRIVER'S LICENSE OR VALID FLORIDA PHOTO ID ALONG WITH YOUR INSURANCE CARD. WE APOLOGIZE IN ADVANCE FOR REQUESTING THESE DOCUMENTS, HOWEVER DUE TO PATIENT INSURANCE FRAUD CASES, WE HAVE NO CHOICE. IT IS YOUR INSURANCE COMPANY THAT IS REQUESTING THIS PROCEDURE. THERE HAVE BEEN PATIENTS USING OTHER PEOPLE'S INSURANCE CARDS FOR TREATMENTS. THIS IS ILLEGAL AND CONSIDERED A VERY SERIOUS CRIME UNDER FEDERAL LAW. THIS ALSO KEEPS YOUR INSURANCE PREMIUMS HIGH.

HELP US STOP PATIENT INSURANCE FRAUD

a death with dignity. This led to the creation of patients' rights groups, intent on protecting each patient's rights to good medical care and informed decision-making. Thus, Americans began to demand more control over their medical treatment.

In 1973, due to pressure from many special interest groups, the American Hospital Association adopted the Patient's Bill of Rights. Medical historian Peter G. Filene elaborates, "First among the twelve points was the right to considerate and respectful care."[21] Part of this document, supported by the American Medical Association, allowed a patient or the patient's family to withdraw any extraordinary treatment.

Prior to the publication of this document, most patients never questioned their physicians. Relying on the doctor's expertise, most patients accepted whatever treatment a physician suggested. As a result of the Patient's Bill of Rights, Hoefler and Kamore suggest that "power has begun to slip away from physicians, leaving patients in a stronger position to control their own medical destinies."[22]

Death, along with medical treatment, has become in the last fifty years a much more complex issue. With the increased visibility and awareness of the issues centered around death and dying, there has also been an increased interest in the way people die. One of the biggest questions that has arisen centers around the fundamental question, Do people have the right to die at a time and in a manner of their own choosing?

CHAPTER 2

EUTHANASIA

While the questions surrounding a person's right to die gained popularity in the late twentieth century, the issue was not a new one. People have debated end-of-life decisions and the dying process for centuries. Much of the controversy has always centered around the dilemma of whether it was better to prolong the life of a person or to assist the dying to end their life. Those supporting these opposite viewpoints have always been adamant in their beliefs and contentions. It is an issue that remains unresolved in the twenty-first century.

Much of the argument about the right to die revolves around the use of euthanasia. Editor of the book *Euthanasia: Opposing Viewpoints* James D. Torr defines euthanasia as "a broad term for mercy killing—taking the life of a hopelessly ill or injured individual in order to end his or her suffering."[23] The word *euthanasia* comes from the Greek language. *Eu* means "good," while *thanatos* means "death." Thus, the word refers to a good death, and for many that means a death that comes about without extended suffering and pain. When the majority of people talk about euthanasia, journalist Sylvia Diane Ledger explains, they are referring to "causing death painlessly to end suffering, especially in cases of incurable, painful diseases."[24]

There are many forms that euthanasia can take. The two major types are active and passive. Active euthanasia is the act of taking steps to end one's own life (suicide) or seeking help do so (assisted suicide). Passive euthanasia, on the other hand, is the act of ending treatment or withdrawing life support, also called "pulling the plug," and allowing the patient to die naturally.

There is also another division: voluntary and involuntary euthanasia. Author Gerald A. Larue elaborates, "Voluntary euthanasia refers to the act of inducing a merciful death in accord with the wishes

Public Opinion on Right-to-Die Laws, 1990 Versus 2005

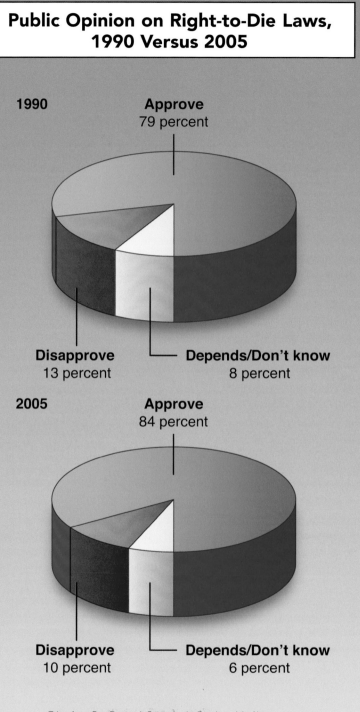

1990

Approve
79 percent

Disapprove
13 percent

Depends/Don't know
8 percent

2005

Approve
84 percent

Disapprove
10 percent

Depends/Don't know
6 percent

Taken from: Pew Research Center for the People and the News.
http://people-press.org/report/266/strong-public-support-for-right-to-die.

and desires of the subject."[25] Involuntary euthanasia, on the other hand, is done without the consent of the patient, such as a family member putting a loved one out of his or her misery by giving an overdose of medication without the dying person's consent. Both involuntary and voluntary euthanasia are considered active forms.

Early American Practices

The different kinds of euthanasia have evolved over the years, along with varying degrees of acceptance. In early America, for instance, *euthanasia* referred primarily to a good death as opposed to a mercy killing.

The term *euthanasia* began to denote mercy killing and physician-administered death beginning in 1873. In that year an early magazine, *Popular Science Monthly*, offered a review that defended the idea of physician-assisted death. Samuel D. Williams noted, "In all cases of hopeless and painful illnesses it should be the recognized duty of the medical attendant, whenever so desired by the patient, to administer chloroform or such other anesthetic . . . so as to destroy consciousness at once, and put the sufferer at once to a quick and painless death."[26] The article was widely circulated throughout the United States and debated by medical professionals.

"A DEFENSIBLE FORM OF EUTHANASIA"

"It is important to distinguish between euthanasia for the dying, of those who have no future, and euthanasia of despair. Suicide for the dying, in unique and rare situations, is a defensible form of euthanasia because there is consent in it." —Ethicist John Bennett.

Quoted in Richard Venus, "When There's No Relief in Sight, Choosing Death Makes Sense," *Dayton Daily News*, November 12, 1998, p. 19A.

The American Medical Association came out vehemently against the article, stating that physicians had no such right to end a life. Association member Isaac N. Quimby responded, "A physician has no right to terminate the life of a patient, even when to prolong that life is to cause the most agonizing tortures."[27] This

stance became the prevailing attitude among physicians throughout the first half of the twentieth century. The American Medical
Association's opposition to euthanasia was shared by medical
groups all over the world.

Interest in Euthanasia

Despite the medical profession's adamant stance against euthanasia, interest in the issue grew among intellectuals in both Great
Britain and the United States. In 1935 a group of English intellectuals headed by playwright George Bernard Shaw, philosopher
and social activist Bertrand Russell, and author H.G. Wells founded the British Euthanasia Society, an organization dedicated to

*Playwright George Bernard Shaw founded the British Euthanasia Society with
other prominent English intellectuals in 1935.*

working toward the legalization of euthanasia in certain instances. Despite support in Great Britain, however, Parliament failed to legalize any form of euthanasia or physician-assisted suicide.

American interest in euthanasia also grew in the 1930s when minister and theologian Charles Francis Potter and New York heiress Ann Mitchell founded the Euthanasia Society of America. The organization, according to author M. Scott Peck, defined euthanasia as "the termination of human life by painless means for the purpose of ending severe physical suffering."[28]

"DEATH IS AN INEVITABILITY, NOT A RIGHT"

"The concept that an individual has the right to die is rejected on the basis that death is an inevitability, not a right. It is argued that the rejection of values, such as the sanctity of life and the intrinsic value of life, and the acceptance of euthanasia and assisted suicide erode the moral and social foundations of society."
—Ethics journalist Sylvia Diane Ledger.

Sylvia Diane Ledger, "Euthanasia and Assisted Suicide: There Is an Alternative," *Ethics and Medicine*, July 1, 2007.

Both of the society's founders, however, were also strong supporters of eugenics, a science based on the improvement of a race or breed by controlling the mating process. Potter and Mitchell expanded the definition to include the belief that the Caucasian race was superior to other races. Those who advocated this belief recommended that African Americans and Native Americans, for example, should be not only banned from "good" society but, in many cases, completely eliminated or killed. Their goal, authors Michael S. Lief and H. Mitchell Caldwell explain, was "to attempt to strengthen the gene pool by weeding out persons deemed mentally, physically or genetically inferior."[29]

Genocide or Euthanasia?

Belief in eugenics and the misuse of euthanasia reached its greatest heights in Nazi Germany under the leadership of Adolf Hitler. Hitler's program began on September 1, 1939, with a decree titled "Order for the Destruction of Lives Which Are Unworthy of

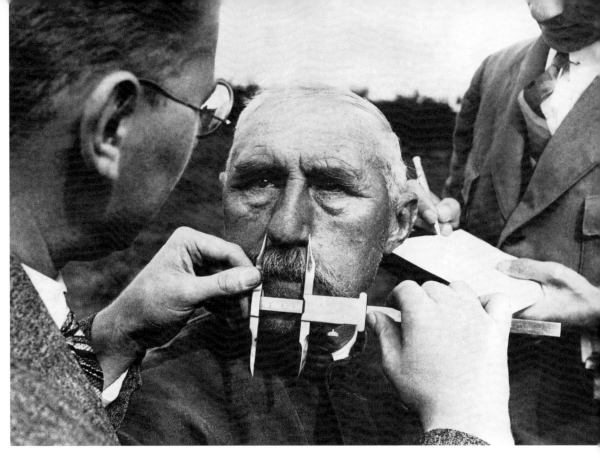

A Nazi official measures a man's face to calculate his "racial purity." The Nazis used euthanasia to get rid of "undesirable" members of the population such as the mentally retarded, homosexuals, and all people of Jewish background.

Being Lived." The first to be euthanized or killed were the mentally retarded and mentally impaired senior citizens, all of whom were in various German hospitals and institutions.

As time passed, Hitler's definition of the "unworthy" expanded to include all people of Jewish background, homosexuals, and Gypsies. Eleven million people were killed during a period of time that has come to be known as the Holocaust. Euthanasia had, in this instance, become genocide, the killing of an entire group of people.

"The Nazi corruption of euthanasia," author Charles F. Mc-Khann contends, "bore no resemblance to the original meaning of the word."[30] Writer Eric Marcus further elaborates, "Hitler used the word euthanasia to describe what was, in fact, the mass murder of . . . men, women, and children, mentally and physically handicapped."[31] Rather than using the word *euthanasia*, many historians use the term *death selection* as more indicative of what the Nazis did during the 1930s and 1940s.

A Revival of Interest

During the height of the Nazi regime and for some years afterward, euthanasia movements around the world lost momentum. Journalist Edward J. Larson explains, "Linking euthanasia to Nazism discredited the practice in the United States."[32] The Euthanasia Society of America particularly came under stern criticism when one of its founders actually suggested that disabled American soldiers be euthanized on their return from Europe and the Pacific.

EUTHANASIA WOULD CAUSE TRAGEDY

"I believe euthanasia lies outside the commonly held life-centered values of the West and cannot be allowed without incurring great social and personal tragedy." —Former surgeon general C. Everett Koop.

Quoted in William H. Colby, *Unplugged: Reclaiming Our Right to Die in America.* New York: AMACOM, 2006, p. 185.

Despite the setbacks, the American euthanasia movement revived in the 1960s and 1970s as public interest was generated in the whole concept of death and dying. Acceding to public pressure, the group revised its philosophy to focus on the rights of terminally ill patients and their right to decide when and how to end their lives. In 1974 the organization changed its name to the less sinister-sounding Society for the Right to Die. An offshoot of the main organization, the Euthanasia Education Fund, became Concern for the Dying and provided educational material to those who were facing the dying process.

Derek Humphry and the Hemlock Society

The American euthanasia and right-to-die movements gained further momentum because of self-educated journalist Derek Humphry. Humphry became interested in euthanasia when his wife, Jean, was diagnosed with terminal breast cancer. After

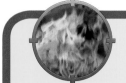

Final Exit

The writings of Hemlock Society founder Derek Humphry have been very controversial. In addition to his first book, *Jean's Way*, which told the story of his wife's death, Humphrey's book *Let Me Die Before I Wake* was published in 1981. It focused on Humphry's support of euthanasia and the choices available to terminally ill patients. Another book, *Final Exit*, followed in 1991. "Final exit" referred to ending one's life by suicide.

In *Final Exit* Humphry outlines specific steps a patient can take to end his life. He gives detailed information on suicide by carbon monoxide and by various medications. It is a step-by-step do-it-yourself book on planning and executing a painless death. Humphry explains, "*Final Exit* is aimed at helping the public and the health profession achieve death with dignity for those who desire to plan for it." The book became an immediate best seller. In addition to American publication, the book was eventually translated into dozens of languages and sold abroad.

Humphrey's books have been criticized by right-to-life organizations, the medical profession, and most organized religions. In fact, critics called one of his books the "suicide cookbook" and condemned him for writing such explicit material.

Derek Humphry, *Final Exit: The Practicalities of Self-Deliverance and Assisted Suicide for the Dying*. Eugene, OR: Hemlock Society, 1991, p. 19.

discussing all options with her, and with her complete agreement, he decided to put an end to her suffering. Humphry was able to obtain a prescription for a heavy sedative, or barbiturate, from a young physician. Sometime later, he mixed the drugs with coffee and gave it to his wife, who willingly drank it down. A short time later, she went to sleep and quietly died. The year was 1973.

By assisting in his wife's death, Humphry had committed a crime, as he recounts in his book *Final Exit:* "I committed the crime of assisting a suicide, the penalty for which in Britain where I was living at the time, is up to fourteen years imprisonment."[33] He was investigated by Scotland Yard but not charged with a crime. The police pressured him to release the name of the physician, but Humphry refused to name him. The matter was eventually dropped.

Following Jean's death Humphry remarried and, together with his new wife, wrote *Jean's Way*, a book describing his first wife's death. The book was widely read and received good reviews. Humphry later moved to the United States and worked for the *Los Angeles Times*. His book was immensely popular, and he became a leading and very vocal supporter of euthanasia and the right to die. These topics soon became his passion and his priority.

In 1980 Humphry founded the Hemlock Society and established its national headquarters in Oregon. The organization takes its name from the drink used by the ancient Greeks to commit suicide. The Hemlock Society advocated that its members live a good life and die a good death. The organization quickly grew to a membership of over forty thousand by 1993. In the beginning the society offered actual how-to information for those considering suicide because of terminal illness. After

Derek Humphry is a strong supporter of euthanasia and the right to die. He founded the Hemlock Society in 1980, which advocated that its members live a good life and die a good death.

Humphry's retirement, the organization took on a more conservative approach, stressing instead the need for public education about the need for legal reforms and legalization of euthanasia. It is now called Compassion and Choices in Dying.

Religious Views

From the beginning organizations such as the Hemlock Society and the Euthanasia Society of America had to contend with criticism and opposition from a wide variety of sources. The predominant source of opposition was and remains organized religion. And within religion, the loudest and most influential voice has always been the Roman Catholic Church. A pastoral letter titled "Living and Dying Well" was issued by the Catholic bishops of Washington and Oregon in 1991. The letter reflects the view of the Catholic Church, as well as that of most other churches: "Euthanasia is a lethal, violent, and unacceptable way of terminating care for the infirm."[34]

The majority of Protestant faiths, including Baptist, Episcopal, Lutheran, Methodist, Presbyterian, and many others, agree with the Catholic doctrine. The Baptist Church's 1990 "Resolution on Death and Dying," for instance, reads: "We believe life

CRUELTY TO HUMANS

"No decent human being would allow an animal to suffer without putting it out of its misery. It is only to human beings that human beings are so cruel as to allow them to live on in pain, in hopelessness, in living death, without moving a muscle to help them." —Science fiction writer Isaac Asimov.

Quoted in Joni Eareckson Tada, *When Is It Right to Die?* Grand Rapids, MI: Zondervan, 1992, p. 56.

and death belong in the hands of God. . . . We oppose euthanasia . . . [and] feel the answer is to be found in faith, endurance, and communication with God."[35]

The Jewish, Islamic, Buddhist, and Hindu faiths all prohibit euthanasia as well. These religions all agree that there is no justification, not even severe suffering, for taking a person's life.

The Catholic Church Opposes Legalized Euthanasia

The majority of mainstream churches firmly oppose euthanasia. The strongest critic is perhaps the Roman Catholic Church. In 1980 Pope John Paul II issued a Declaration on Euthanasia as part of the church's Doctrine of the Faith. Many other denominations soon followed with their own critique of euthanasia. A part of the pope's declaration is printed below:

> Most people regard life as something sacred and hold that no one may dispose of it at will, but believers see in life something greater, namely a gift of God's love, which they are called upon to preserve and make fruitful. . . .
>
> None can make an attempt on the life of an innocent person without opposing God's love for that person, without violating a fundamental right, and therefore, without committing a crime. . . .
>
> Everyone has a duty to lead his or her life in accordance with God's plan.

Intentionally causing one's own death, or suicide, is therefore equally as wrong as murder: such an action on the part of a person is to be considered as a rejection of God's sovereignty and loving plan. . . .

By euthanasia is understood an action or an omission which of itself or by intention causes death, in order that all suffering may in this way be eliminated. . . .

It is necessary to state firmly . . . that nothing and no one can in any way permit the killing of an innocent human being, whether a fetus, an embryo, an infant or an adult, an older person, or one suffering from an incurable disease, or a person who is dying. Furthermore, no one is permitted to ask for this act of killing. For it is a question of the violation of a divine law.

Quoted in United States Catholic Bishops, "Declaration on Euthanasia." www.usccb.org/profile/tdocs/euthanasia.shtml.

"According to Islamic law," for instance, "God is the creator of life," author David Cundiff explains. "Consequently, persons do not own their own lives and have no right to end them or to ask others to do so."[36]

The Unitarian Universalist Association, a religious group that includes the Unitarian and Universalist churches, is the only

In 2007 Pope Benedict XVI signs the apostolic exhortation urging, among other things, that Catholic lawmakers oppose laws favoring euthanasia.

mainstream religion that supports voluntary euthanasia. Their doctrine states, "Be it further resolved that Unitarian Universalists advocate the right to self-determination in dying, and the release from civil and criminal penalties of those who, under proper safeguards, act to honor the right of terminally ill patients to select the time of their own deaths."[37]

The Slippery Slope

Adding their voices to the criticism of using or legalizing euthanasia are countless other critics. Many opponents of euthanasia fear that legalizing such mercy killing would lead the United States toward adopting some of the Nazi-style killing of the elderly and the socially disfavored. Most of these critics call this the "slippery slope." Writers Hoefler and Kamore explain:

> One step onto the . . . [euthanasia] ramp would cause
> society to slide downward uncontrollably, to the point

where euthanasia would be administered without consent in some cases and where potential candidates would feel pressured (and maybe even obliged) to choose the euthanasia option rather than burden family and friends by prolonging the inevitable.[38]

Catholic bishop Joseph Sullivan agrees. He says:

> Once the respect for human life is so low that an innocent person may be killed directly, even at his own request,

Disability rights activists picket the home of Dr. Jack Kevorkian, called "Dr. Death," for his advocacy of assisted suicide. They fear that the legalization of assisted suicide will be the "slippery slope" that could lead to the involuntary euthanization of the disabled.

compulsory euthanasia will necessarily be near. This could lead easily to killing all charity patients, the aged who are in public care, wounded soldiers, all deformed children, the mentally afflicted, and so on. Before long, the danger would be at the door of every citizen.[39]

Proponents of euthanasia, however, dismiss these arguments as invalid. They are quick to point out that the atrocities that happened in Germany were done under a dictatorship, not in a democracy. Nor were the killings done with anyone's consent. Journalist Richard Venus elaborates, "What was missing [during the Holocaust] . . . was the element that is crucial to a moral form of euthanasia—that of fully informed, uncoerced consent."[40]

Other proponents cite the need to alleviate suffering as being of the utmost importance. Daniel Callahan, cofounder of the Hastings Institute, a nonprofit bioethics research group, argues, "Given . . . our mutual agreement that human suffering should be avoided if possible and relieved when it occurs—how can anyone morally oppose physician-assisted suicide [or euthanasia] to save someone from it?"[41]

Author Marcus concludes, "By denying the terminally ill the right to seek aid in dying from a doctor, we force lay people to act on their own, risking additional pain and suffering in the event the assisted suicide is botched."[42] We also force the dying to use violent means. Many believe that competent terminally ill patients should have the right to enlist a willing doctor to help end their life. By denying this right, proponents say, we prolong both their lives and their suffering.

Various forms of euthanasia have been practiced throughout human history, with varying degrees of medical and public support. The growth of the right-to-die movement and the various euthanasia societies in the latter half of the twentieth century raised new questions about human suffering. The controversy became even more complicated over the issue of assisted suicide.

ASSISTED SUICIDE

The most controversial right-to-die issue centers on the concept of assisted suicide and physician-assisted suicide. Thousands of people help loved ones die around the world, but the majority of these occurrences are not reported. They take place quietly in the homes of the terminally ill as family members and friends take active steps to bring on the death of someone they love. Most assisted deaths, as a result, go undiscovered and are usually officially ruled as natural deaths.

Many doctors and nurses have also quietly practiced assisted suicide. In fact, a survey taken of nearly one thousand nurses showed that nearly 16 percent had helped hasten a death. A study done in 1988 by the Massachusetts Medical Society reported that a significant number of physicians across the United States had also received requests for assisted suicide. Approximately 6 percent had assisted in patients' deaths. A San Francisco poll of local physicians found the percentage much higher: 53 percent of surveyed doctors reported that they had helped AIDS patients die by prescribing lethal doses of narcotics. These assisted suicides have also gone unreported for years.

Whether done openly or secretly, assisted suicide has been condemned by right-to-life groups for decades. Right-to-life advocates believe that life is sacred and should not be shortened in any circumstance. Arguments for and against assisted suicide abound. Right-to-die advocate Robert T. Hall elaborates on behalf of those who favor assisted suicide: "The most compelling argument in favor of physician-assisted suicide has always been the one based upon the fact that some conditions are so intolerable that the only relief is death."[43]

Opponents of physician-assisted suicide counter that if assisted suicide were legalized, then many patients who were simply depressed or mentally unstable would take advantage of the law and commit suicide. Author Eric Marcus summarizes, "Assisted suicide is one of the most fraught emotional, political, and moral issues of our time."[44] Opinions vary from those who wholeheartedly support it to those who bitterly condemn it; there seems to be little middle ground.

What Is Assisted Suicide?

The word *suicide* comes from the Latin words *cida*, meaning "to kill," and *sui*, meaning "oneself." In an assisted suicide, another person, whether a physician or a loved one, helps in the death of an individual. In a physician-assisted suicide, that person is a doctor, who either acts on the patient's behalf or provides the means for a patient to kill him- or herself.

Theorists and right-to-die supporters contend that assisted suicide is far different from "ordinary" suicide. Writer Stephen

Many supporters of physician-assisted suicide believe that the terminally ill are suicidal due to the hopelessness of their condition, not because they are depressed.

Jamison explains: "Suicide ends a life that could continue, and implies irrationality rooted in an identifiable mental condition that may be treatable with proper therapy and medications."[45] Assisted suicide is different in that it involves a rational decision to end a life of suffering.

DO NO HARM

"Physicians have a fundamental obligation to do no harm. . . . Physician assisted suicide is fundamentally incompatible with the physician's role as healer, would be difficult or impossible to control, and would pose serious societal risks."   —American Medical Association.

JAMA, "Physician Assisted Suicide," 1992, pp. 2,229–33.

Assisted suicide also involves consent. This kind of suicide has also been called rational suicide. Unlike irrational suicide that occurs in depression and other mental illnesses, rational suicide is a decision made by a terminally ill patient who is of sound mind. Two major themes are involved: the desire to avoid unnecessary suffering and the desire to exercise self-determination by making a rational decision to end one's life. Many supporters of assisted suicide contend that suicidal thoughts are not always symptoms of depression and may instead be reflective of the hopelessness and suffering felt by many terminally ill patients.

Rational suicide involves those individuals with a terminal or debilitating illness who, in an effort to end their physical and mental suffering, ask a physician to prescribe a lethal dose of medication. They are not asking the doctor to end their lives, but to make the means available to them for doing so. Such patients might include those with terminal cancer; severe multiple sclerosis; AIDS; and end-stage lung, liver, or kidney disease. These diseases are all characterized by severe pain and the deterioration of bodily functions and mental capacities.

Opponents of assisted suicide are quick to respond. Right-to-life supporters argue that any self-inflicted death, with or without help, is an irrational act. They believe that life is sacred and should not be shortened, whatever the circumstances. Former Penn State University professor Robert A. Walker explains: "The people who support the 'above all, sustain life' position are not insensitive to the situations in which people might be in severe pain or losing their minds. . . . What they understand is that suffering is part of life and often brings family together."[46]

Why Physician-Assisted Suicide?

Despite knowing that assisted suicide is against the law, countless people approach their physicians asking for an end to their suffering. In fact, the vast majority of people who seek an assisted suicide are those with terminal illnesses that are accompanied by severe pain and other suffering. Sylvia Diane Ledger, a registered nurse and lecturer at the Royal London Hospital in Great Britain, elaborates: "Ongoing, unrelieved suffering gives rise to loss of hope and despair. The patient whose symptoms have not/cannot be adequately controlled may ask for euthanasia or assisted suicide to escape their suffering and/or restore their dignity."[47] Her opinion is supported by thousands of hospice professionals who have heard such requests.

Many terminal illnesses are accompanied by increasing weakness that often keeps patients confined to bed. As a result, patients often do not have the physical ability to end their own lives. Thus, they must turn elsewhere. Writer Stephen Jamison summarizes: "You should not have to choose between pain and death. Until medicine can re-establish its promise, or indeed guarantee, a more gentle death . . . the dying will seek whatever alternatives are possible."[48]

Most members of the various right-to-die societies strongly advocate assisted suicide. They firmly contend that each person should be able to die with dignity in a manner and time of their own choosing. Journalist Simonne Liberty opines:

> I believe a person should be able to have the choice to die with dignity. Why force a person to continue on in pain and misery when there is no hope for recovery. That constitutes a form of cruel and unusual punishment. . . . No one should make a dying person suffer needlessly,

Joseph Fletcher

Joseph Francis Fletcher is acknowledged as the father of modern biomedical ethics and a champion of physician-assisted suicide. Editor Robert F. Weir elaborates: "No single individual championed the cause of physician-administered death more than Joseph Fletcher. . . . He defended the morality of euthanasia as an act of mercy for patients who have no reasonable hope of recovery and for whom narcotics cannot relieve pain."

In 1954 Fletcher authored the book *Morals and Medicine*, the first non-Catholic treatment of medical ethics in the care of the terminally ill. His basic premise was that people should have a choice in all decisions, including the right to die.

Another book, *Situational Ethics*, was penned in 1966. In this book, Fletcher wrote: "We need to educate people to the idea that the quality of life is more important than mere length of life. Our cultural tradition holds that life has absolute value, but that is really not good enough anymore. Sometimes no life is better."

Robert F. Weir, *Physician-Assisted Suicide*. Bloomington: Indiana University Press, 1997, p. 52.

Quoted in Answers.com, "Biography: Joseph Francis Fletcher." www.answers.com/topic/joseph-fletcher.

for a prolonged period, if that person asks for a premature death to end the suffering sooner. It should be an individual's personal choice.[49]

The Suicide Doctor

The issue of physician-assisted suicide was put to its sternest test with the rise to popularity of the "suicide doctor," Jack Kevorkian. When people think about mercy killing or physician-assisted suicide, it is his name that immediately comes to most minds. Kevorkian has, in fact, admitted that he has helped over one hundred people die. Heavily publicized, he has been very vocal in his support of physician-assisted suicide. Writer Tamara L. Roleff summarizes Kevorkian's importance: "Kevorkian changed assisted suicide from a little-discussed practice into a national issue argued in front of the United States Supreme Court."[50]

A pathologist by training, Kevorkian became interested in the dying process while still a medical resident. After graduating

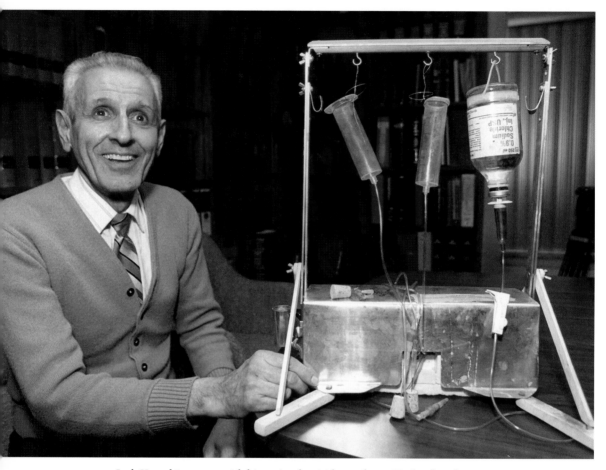

Jack Kevorkian poses with his assisted-suicide machine. He developed two machines: One machine delivered carbon monoxide, a lethal gas, to the patient via a mask; the other machine combined a sedative, a muscle relaxer, and potassium chloride, a drug that paralyzes the heart muscles. The patient had to activate both machines.

from medical school in 1952, Kevorkian developed an interest in prisoners on death row. After working in the prison system for a number of years, his belief that the current methods of execution, including hanging and the gas chamber, were barbaric led him to an interest in more humane forms of death, such as death by lethal injection. After spending time in the Netherlands, where euthanasia and assisted suicide were common, he returned to the United States intent on pursuing his interest in euthanasia. He wrote, "Back in Michigan and inspired by my visit to the Netherlands, I decided to take the risky step of assisting terminal patients in committing suicide."[51]

After finding little support from oncologists (doctors who treat cancer), Kevorkian began work on a machine that would allow a patient to end his or her life in a merciful way. He called his machine the "Mercitron." It delivered carbon monoxide, a lethal gas, to the patient via a mask, causing death within five to ten minutes. He later developed another machine, which was dubbed the "Thanatron," or "death machine." The combination of a sedative, muscle relaxer, and potassium chloride, a drug that paralyzes the heart muscles, would provide, he thought, a humane and merciful death for those suffering from terminal illness. Both machines had to be activated by the patient.

HONOR THE REQUEST

"When terminally ill patients request assistance in dying because of their suffering, and their request meets commonly endorsed safeguards, their request should be honored." —Eric J. Cassell, professor of public health at Cornell University.

Quoted in Euthanasia—ProCon.org, "Is a Physician Ever Obligated to Help a Patient Die?" www.euthanasiaprocon.org/helpdie/html.

Unable to put his machine into practice because of controversy and lack of interest, Kevorkian appeared on national television on the *Phil Donahue Show*. This finally brought him the notoriety he sought. He soon had his first patient. Janet Adkins had been diagnosed with Alzheimer's disease, an illness that gradually leads to mental deterioration and physical wasting. Not wanting to put herself or her family through the ordeal of the disease, Adkins contacted Kevorkian, who agreed to help her die. Adkins met with the doctor and proceeded with plans to end her life. She left a note exonerating Kevorkian of any blame: "I don't choose to put my family or myself through the agony of this terrible disease."[52] Her death and that of a number of other people who contacted Kevorkian followed.

Not long after news of these deaths gained worldwide attention in 1991, the Michigan Medical Association and the state government took away Kevorkian's medical license. Despite the lack of medical credentials, Kevorkian continued to help patients end their lives. Unable to obtain the necessary drugs for injection, he switched to the use of his carbon monoxide machine. Brought to trial on three different occasions on charges of assisting a suicide, Michigan juries repeatedly found him not guilty of any crime.

Despite the not guilty verdicts, the state of Michigan eventually passed a law that put a permanent ban on assisted suicide on September 1, 1998. Jack Kevorkian waited only two weeks after the law went into effect to test the legality of it.

The Netherlands

In addition to Oregon, there are only three other places that openly and legally allow physicians to assist in the deaths of their patients: Switzerland, Belgium, and the Netherlands. Most of the attention, however, is focused on the Netherlands, where physician-assisted suicide has been commonly practiced for over thirty years but only recognized as legal in the last six.

The Dutch Voluntary Euthanasia Society was founded in the late 1970s and began advocating physician-assisted suicide. The organization quickly gained widespread public support. Not long thereafter, the Royal Dutch Society for the Promotion of Medicine set up guidelines for physician-assisted suicide. Under Dutch law, the doctor must be convinced the patient's request is voluntary and well considered. The physician must also document that the patient is facing unrelenting suffering. After consultation with another physician, the original doctor can proceed with the assisted suicide.

It is estimated that nearly 20 percent of physicians in the Netherlands have helped patients end their suffering. In 1995, for instance, there were over one hundred thousand deaths in the country; thirty-six hundred of those were as a result of physician-assisted suicide or euthanasia, accounting for a small percentage of deaths in the Netherlands. Physicians primarily use injected barbiturates, or sedatives, to induce unconsciousness; this is followed by the use of a muscle relaxer to cause death.

Kevorkian's Downfall

Kevorkian's downfall came in November 1998, not long after he appeared on CBS's *60 Minutes*. During the show, Kevorkian allowed the television crew to film the actual death of one of his patients, fifty-two-year-old Thomas Youk. Youk had Lou Gehrig's disease, a disease that renders the patient incapable of swallowing, moving, and breathing properly. Youk could not press the injector button, so Kevorkian did it for him. He told television viewers that this was the first time he, himself, had pushed the button for a patient.

LEGALIZED ASSISTED DYING ENSURES QUALITY CARE

"Legal change with strict control would reduce the current problems of inappropriate aid-in-dying by physicians and significant others and ensure quality of care for the dying." —Right-to-die supporter Stephen Jamison.

Stephen Jamison, *Final Acts of Love: Families, Friends, and Assisted Dying.* New York: G.P. Putnam's Sons, 1995, p. 250.

Kevorkian also readily admitted that he wanted prosecutors to charge him with a crime because he believed that, by winning in court, he could make assisted suicide legal. He got his wish—he was quickly charged by Michigan prosecutors with murder and brought to trial. A Michigan jury convicted the seventy-year-old physician of second-degree murder. Judge Jessica Cooper, in speaking to Kevorkian, stated: "You had the audacity to go on national television, show the world what you did, and dare the legal system to stop you. Well sir, consider yourself stopped."[53]

The reaction to Kevorkian's conviction was immediate. The American Medical Association condemned him, calling him "a self-admitted zealot killing another human being to advance his own interests and ego-driven urge to martyrdom."[54] Even some of the right-to-die organizations that had earlier supported Kevorkian's work began to denounce the Michigan doctor.

Jack Kevorkian received a sentence of ten to twenty-five years in a Michigan prison for the second-degree murder of a terminally ill man.

Despite the widespread criticism of Kevorkian's actions, Youk's family continued to praise him, as did Mike Wallace, longtime CBS newsman and the man who interviewed Kevorkian during the Youk televised program. Wallace offered his opinion: "He's a decent and compassionate man who tried to help people get out of the suffering of their lives. Kevorkian's incarceration amounts to cruel and unusual punishment."[55]

On April 13, 1999, Cooper sentenced Kevorkian to ten to twenty-five years in prison. He served eight years and was released on parole in June 2007. The terms of his release included his promise that he would not assist in anyone's death. His attorney stated: "Dr. Kevorkian will follow all conditions of his parole. He pledges not to participate in any assisted end-of-life events, but he will resume his passionate advocacy for the legalization of physician-guided termination of life related to irreversible or incurable disease, pain, and suffering."[56]

Oregon Death with Dignity

Kevorkian had developed his suicide machines to challenge the laws against assisted suicide by actively helping people to die. Concerned that Kevorkian's blatant disregard of the law would have a negative impact on public opinion, other supporters

Attorney Eli Stutsman, lead drafter of the Oregon Death with Dignity Act, speaks to reporters following a federal judge's ruling upholding physician-assisted suicide in 2002.

of assisted suicide distanced themselves from his controversial actions. Instead they chose to work within the law. Encouraged by public opinion polls that indicated over 60 percent of the population favored physician-assisted suicide, right-to-die groups in a number of states proposed legislation that would legalize assisted suicide.

While efforts failed in California and Washington, assisted suicide supporters were more successful in Oregon. In the early 1990s, concerned citizens formed Oregon Death with Dignity for the purpose of passing a law that would allow dying patients to make and control their own end-of-life decisions. Measure 16, the Oregon Death with Dignity Act, was placed before the voters in November 1994 and passed by a slim margin of 51 percent to 49 percent.

The new law was immediately challenged. On November 23, 1994, two weeks before it was to take effect, a suit was filed in U.S. District Court, delaying the law's implementation. The main opposition to the law came from lawmakers and right-to-life organizations. The Oregon Death with Dignity organization successfully defended the law in multiple cases in both state and federal courts.

The Oregon legislature brought the issue before the voters again in 1997. Oregon voters supported the act by an even wider margin; 60 percent voted to retain the law. Physician-assisted suicide became a legal alternative for terminally ill patients in Oregon in late 1997. According to the Oregon Department of Human Resources, "The Death with Dignity Act allows terminally ill Oregon residents to obtain and use prescriptions from their physicians for self-administered, lethal medications."[57]

The second passage of the law, however, did not end the legal or governmental challenges. In the late 1990s, Representative Henry J. Hyde, chair of the Judiciary Committee, attempted to overturn the act by introducing the Lethal Drug Abuse Prevention Act of 1998 to the U.S. House of Representatives. According to writer Philip King, "The purpose of the Act was to prohibit the dispensing or distribution of a controlled substance for the purpose of causing, or assisting in causing, the suicide of any individual."[58] Hearings on the bill were held in July 1998, but the act never reached the House of Representatives. Other efforts by the Senate also failed to overturn the Oregon Death with Dignity Act. The issue was put to rest in January 2006 when the U.S. Supreme Court upheld the act in *Gonzales v. Oregon*.

Guidelines in Oregon

Between the implementation of the Oregon law in 1998 and the end of 2005, nearly 250 patients used the law to hasten their deaths. This figure averages out to about 1 of every 1,000 deaths in that state.

To use the Death with Dignity law, patients must be eighteen years of age or older, an Oregon resident, and have the ability to

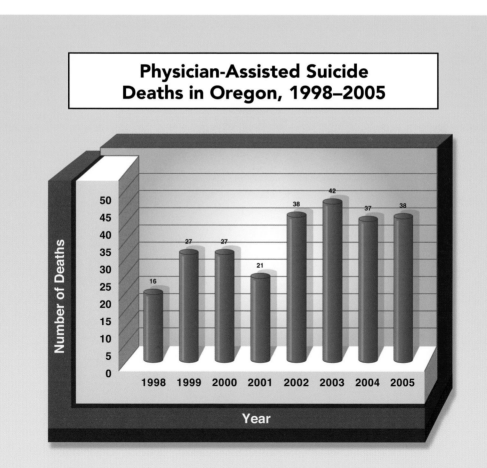

Physician-Assisted Suicide Deaths in Oregon, 1998–2005

Taken from: Eighth Annual Report on Oregon's Death with Dignity Act. www.oregon.gov/DHS/ph/pas/docs/year8.pdf.

communicate their own health care decisions. They must have a terminal illness with a life expectation of less than six months and must make the request in writing.

Proponents of the Oregon law claim that the Death with Dignity Act does not legalize euthanasia. Legislators tried to counter the fears of those who opposed assisted suicide by ensuring that physicians could not assist the patient other than by prescribing the medication. King summarizes: "One of the key elements under the Oregon statute that makes assisted suicide more acceptable to the public is the patient must take the medication with-

A panel representing the right-to-die organization Compassion in Dying discusses Oregon's physician-assisted suicide law. The panelists include Dr. Al Willeford (second from right), who has liver cancer.

out help from a third party. This feature lessens the possibility of undue influence or other influences upon a person's choice to end their life."[59] The law is also appealing to those with terminal illness because it enables such patients to die in the presence of their loved ones instead of in hospital isolation.

"FROM BAD TO GOOD"

"Once killing is redefined from bad to good, the protective guidelines for assisted suicide . . . are also quickly redefined . . . as obstacles to overcome. Then they are attacked, ignored, reinterpreted, while potential violations go essentially uninvestigated—to the point where they eventually become irrelevant." —Wesley Smith, consultant to the International Task Force on Euthanasia.

Quoted in Euthanasia—ProCon.org, "Would Legalizing Voluntary Euthanasia and Assisted Suicide Create a Slippery Slope to Involuntary Euthanasia?" www.euthanasia procon.org/slipperyslope.html.

Thus, an Oregon physician can legally prescribe drugs to assist a terminally ill person to take his or her own life. Not all terminally ill patients take advantage of the law; many choose to die naturally without the aid of assisted suicide options. Also, there has not been any indication of abuse of the law. For example, no evidence has been brought forth to suggest that individuals who have nonterminal illnesses have been given life-ending prescriptions. Because of the compliance with the law, the majority of people in Oregon support the legislation. In nearby Washington, the supporters of assisted suicide continue to work toward its legalization. In the meantime, a Washington physician who assists someone to die would be guilty of a felony, punishable by five years in prison and a ten-thousand-dollar fine.

Autonomy

Right-to-die supporters used the success of Oregon's Death with Dignity law to challenge further the legality of laws in other states that prohibited physician-assisted suicide. They based their arguments on the American Constitution's guarantee of autonomy. Writer Charles F. McKhann elaborates, "Personal autonomy is the

Early Uses of Assisted Suicide

State courts have been inconsistent in their rulings on assisted suicide. Many courts have been lenient toward those who assist a loved one to die, especially in those cases where the loved one was suffering or in extreme pain. Other courts ruled more stringently against the accused. Each case has been handled separately; even those cases heard in the same state have met with different outcomes.

In 1935 a physician named Harold Blazer of Colorado was accused of murder when he used chloroform to end the life of his thirty-year-old daughter. His daughter, the size of a five-year-old child, had spinal meningitis and was suffering pain and other debilitating symptoms. He was arrested, charged, and then acquitted of all charges.

Acquitting such physicians was the rule for much of the twentieth century. Hermann N. Sanders of New Hampshire, for instance, assisted in the death of his terminally ill patient and was acquitted of all wrongdoing, as was Vincent Montemarano of Long Island, who injected a fatal dosage of drugs into a patient with incurable throat cancer. In the case of Sanders, 600 of the 650 residents of his hometown signed a petition of confidence in him that helped in his exoneration.

The courts were also lenient toward family members and friends who helped end the life of the terminally ill. Louis Greenfield used chloroform on his severely retarded son, who, while not terminally ill, was in a near vegetative state. Greenfield was acquitted, as was Carol Paight, who shot her terminally ill policeman father. Even John Stephens of Atlanta, after bashing his sixty-year-old aunt in the head to end her agony from terminal cancer, was acquitted.

There were exceptions, however, to this leniency. In 1986 Joseph Hassman of New Jersey was charged in the death of his eighty-year-old mother who had Alzheimer's disease. He was found guilty, sentenced to two years probation, and fined ten thousand dollars. He also was ordered to do four hundred hours of community service. And in 1985 Roswell Gilbert, seventy-five, of Fort Lauderdale was sentenced to life in prison for shooting his wife, who had Alzheimer's.

liberty to make decisions for oneself, free from outside influence and constraints, and the capacity to act upon those decisions."[60]

For many years the supporters of physician-assisted suicide had argued that patients had the right to end their lives because of the Constitution's guarantee of this liberty. Journalists Edd Doerr and M.L. Tina Stevens explain the reasoning behind this argument: "The right of a competent, terminally ill patient to end his or her life with the aid of a physician is one of the most important liberties protected by the due process clause of the Fourteenth Amendment."[61] The due process clause refers to the fact that the government must respect *all* of a person's rights. Supporters of assisted suicide interpret this to include the right to die.

These rights to liberty, due process, and autonomy were first challenged in the mid-1960s in the case of *Griswold v. Connecticut* heard by the U.S. Supreme Court. The Court, in this case, ruled that states could not prohibit the use of contraception by

Estelle Griswold, executive director of the Planned Parenthood League, stands outside a Planned Parenthood Center in New Haven, Connecticut, in 1963. The landmark case Griswold v. Connecticut *legalized the use of contraception by adults and served as a basis for assisted suicide advocates in their legal battle.*

mature adults. Then came *Roe v. Wade* in 1973, in which the Supreme Court stated that a Texas law that made abortion a crime was unconstitutional. The Court used an individual's autonomy and resulting right to privacy as the centerpiece in their arguments of both cases. Supporters of physician-assisted suicide used these arguments to assert that a patient's right to privacy extended to include end-of-life decisions. Opponents, on the other hand, assert that these constitutional clauses do not give anyone the right to end his or her life through assisted suicide or any other means.

The Law Is Challenged

In the late 1990s the right-to-die organizations became involved in a court case that challenged the laws against assisted suicide. In the case of *Compassion in Dying v. Washington*, the group Compassion in Dying supported three terminally ill patients and their physicians in the state of Washington. They were challenging a Washington statute that made assisted suicide a criminal act. Group member James Browning contended, "We believe the cases . . . provide strong general support for our conclusion that a liberty interest in controlling the time and manner of one's death is protected by the Due Process Clause of the 14th Amendment."[62]

The Ninth Circuit Court of Appeals ruled in March 1996 for the patients and their physicians. In the decision Judge Stephen Reinhardt stated:

> Recognition of any right creates the possibility of abuse. The slippery slope fears of Roe's [*Roe v Wade*] opponents have, of course, not materialized. The legalization of abortion has not undermined our commitment to life generally; nor, as some predicted, has it led to widespread infanticide. Similarly there is no reason to believe that legalizing assisted suicide will lead to the horrific consequences its opponents suggest.[63]

Supreme Court Challenge

The ruling in this case was later appealed to the U.S. Supreme Court and heard in 1997. It was paired with a similar case out of

Supreme Court Chief Justice William Rehnquist wrote the opinion in the ruling that upheld Washington's ban on physician-assisted suicide in 1997.

the state of New York. After reviewing the two cases, the Court ruled that no such liberty to end life existed in the Constitution. The Court also found that Washington's ban on physician-assisted suicide was legal. Chief Justice William Rehnquist wrote the opinion: "The history of the law's treatment of assisted suicide in this country has been and continues to be one of the rejection of nearly all efforts to permit it. That being the case, our decisions lead us to conclude that the asserted right to assist in committing suicide is not a fundamental liberty protected by the Due Process Clause."[64]

Despite the ruling, the Supreme Court justices gave the impression in their summations that it was generally supportive of a patient's right to die. Chief Justice Rehnquist, writing for the Court, indicated that the Court hoped that an open debate about physician-assisted suicide would continue.

Visitors line up outside the Supreme Court Building for the opening session of the 1996–1997 term. In 1997 the justices deliberated on whether to create a consitutional amendment giving Americans the right to pursue physician-assisted suicide.

The Debate Continues

Rehnquist's hope that the debate about assisted suicide would continue has been realized. The arguments surrounding the issue continue, often heatedly. The reason for the vehemence is that physician-assisted suicide is a very complex issue. Those who support and those who oppose legalizing assisted suicide have strong reasons for their beliefs and see little room for compromise.

The same kind of strong beliefs and the tendency to avoid compromise has extended to other forms of euthanasia. While assisted suicide is an active form of euthanasia, passive euthanasia has also drawn its share of proponents and opponents. The arguments over the refusal of treatment are nearly as heated as those involving assisted suicide.

REFUSING MEDICAL TREATMENT

While assisted suicide is the most hotly debated form of euthanasia, other kinds of euthanasia have also had their share of contentious arguments. The refusal of lifesaving treatment or the stoppage of treatment, both passive forms of euthanasia, involve several issues. The hospice, or palliative care, approach is seen as a viable and acceptable alternative to physician-assisted suicide because it provides pain management and an end to overtreatment of terminal illness. Right-to-die supporters are adamant that someone who is terminally ill should be able to choose whether to continue treatment or stop it.

Another type of passive euthanasia is the refusal of treatment on religious grounds. These religious groups are, for the most part, exercising their right to practice their religion. This refusal of treatment, however, also is hotly debated as a right-to-die versus right-to-life issue. Right-to-die supporters contend that all mentally competent adults have the right to choose a time and place of their own death. These supporters, for the most part, have no problem with adult members of religious groups' choosing to refuse any form of potentially lifesaving medical treatment. Right-to-life groups and many right-to-die supporters, however, draw the line when it comes to the care of children. They contend that the refusal of treatment that could potentially save a child from a nonterminal illness is a tragedy. A parent who chooses not to obtain medical treatment for his or her child for religious reasons, while protected by law, has been hotly criticized for decades by both groups as well as the medical profession.

Stopping Treatment

An anonymous article in *Atlantic Monthly* in 1957 stated: "If you are very ill, modern medicine can save you. If you are going to die it can prevent you from so doing for a very long time."[65] The article further contended that in many cases, especially those

Cryonics

Not everyone is ready to accept death as the end of life. Scientists have worked for years to develop a method that could preserve the body for possible future reanimation. This science is called cryonics. Cryonics (from the Greek word *kryos*, meaning "cold") is the low-temperature preservation of human beings by means of a freezing process that maintains the body after death. The premise of this practice is that sometime in the distant future, technology will become available that can bring these people back to life. Author James Haley explains, "Advocates of cryonics believe that in the next fifty to two hundred years, scientists will have developed the technology to restore these frozen bodies to life." Critics of the process doubt the feasibility of the plan. Cryobiologist John Bischof of the University of Minnesota states that cryonics is "science fiction at its worst" and has "no hope of reviving dead bodies."

The modern era of cryonics, however, began in 1962 when a Michigan college physics teacher named Robert Ettinger in his book *The Prospect of Immortality* advo-cated the freezing process for extending life into the future. As a result of his work, the American Cryonics Society was founded in 1969. The first actual suspensions were performed in 1974. Writers James Hoefler and Brian Kamore explain the process: "Cryonic suspension . . . involves infusing the body with glycerine, then super-cooling it in a vat of liquid nitrogen." The procedure can only be done after the person is dead.

There are three organizations where this technology is available: The Alcor Life Extension Foundation in Arizona, the Cryonics Institute in Michigan, and the American Cryonics Society in California. There are approximately 180 people in cryonic suspension at these sites. Family members paid exorbitant amounts of money to have their loved ones stored and suspended.

James Haley, ed., *Opposing Viewpoints: Death and Dying.* Farmington Hills, MI: Greenhaven, 2003, p. 150.

Quoted in Monte Reel, "Frozen for the Future," *Washington Post*, July 22, 2002.

James M. Hoefler and Brian E. Kamore, *Deathright: Culture, Medicine, Politics, and the Right to Die.* Boulder, CO: Westview, 1994, p. 8.

involving terminal illnesses, doctors were often guilty of over-treatment despite their patient's wishes to be allowed to die naturally. Over a decade later, as public interest in the dying process intensified, a poll was taken in 1973 to evaluate public opinion about treatment at the end of life. The poll showed that over 60 percent of Americans believed that they should be able to tell their doctors when to stop treatment—to let them die rather than continue treatment. Shortly thereafter, medical experts and ethicists began discussing the right of patients to refuse medical treatment.

"IT IS A DISGRACE"

"It is a disgrace that the majority of our health care providers lack the knowledge and the skills to properly treat pain and other symptoms of terminal disease." —Hospice physician David Cundiff.

David Cundiff, *Euthanasia Is Not the Answer: A Hospice Physician's View.* Totowa, NJ: Humana, 1992, p. 9.

The central question in this discussion was whether continued treatment in terminally ill patients was truly beneficial to the patient. When the average patient suffers from a treatable illness, life support and other extraordinary measures are temporary procedures that are utilized for a short period of time until the patient's body can function on its own. In some conditions, however, such as terminal disease, such measures are viewed differently. They are seen by much of the public and many social commentators as prolonging the inevitable and often causing more suffering than is warranted. Author George M. Burnell concludes: "Dying is no longer a simple matter. . . . There are worse things than dying. . . . You could get stuck with treatments you don't want and procedures that won't let you die in peace."[66]

"Unfortunately, many patients with advanced cancer [and other terminal diseases,]" hospice physician David Cundiff explains, "are needlessly resuscitated and placed on life support systems when there is no reasonable hope of recovery."[67] This

The right to refuse medical treatment becomes a thorny issue when the patient is a child. Edward and Michelle Wernecke's daughter Katie was taken into state custody after they refused radiation in the treatment of her cancer.

happens in many cases because physicians are reluctant to give up; instead they continue aggressive treatment even though a patient's chances of recovery are miniscule. In addition, sometimes families want continued treatment because they are reluctant to give up hope for a miraculous cure. Author Burnell explains, "In the medical setting, busy doctors sometimes continue to treat because the technology is available or because families continue to pressure them and insist that everything possible be done."[68] Many of these patients end up in hospitals or nursing homes, where unwanted and often unnecessary treatments continue endlessly.

The Terminally Ill

Thus, among the primary questions that arise when a patient is diagnosed with a terminal illness are how much treatment that patient should receive and when treatments should be stopped. Norman J. Geisler in his book *Christian Ethics* writes: "Keeping a comatose person who has an incurable disease alive on a machine when he is irreversibly dying is unnecessary. In fact, it could be viewed as unethical. . . . Extraordinary efforts to fight the divinely appointed limits of our mortality are really working in opposition to God."[69]

The use of aggressive treatment was tested in the courts in May 1976. A nursing home patient, Joseph Saikewicz, was sixty-seven years old but had the equivalent of a ten-year-old's intelligence because of severe mental retardation. He was unable to make decisions on his own behalf. When he was diagnosed with leukemia, the question arose as to whether he was a candidate for chemotherapy. A probate court appointed a guardian to decide this issue. It was decided that, for this particular patient, chemotherapy was not an appropriate treatment, primarily

Guardians must often make difficult decisions about the care of individuals unable to make decisions on their own behalf.

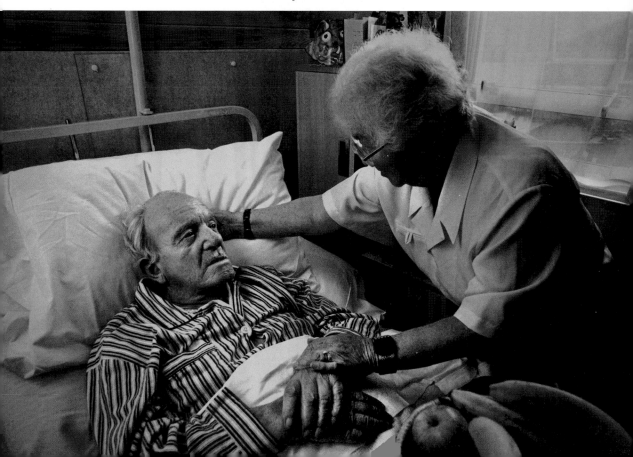

because there was no way to explain to Saikewicz about the treatment's side effects. In addition, the guardian realized that the patient would have to be physically restrained during treatment, thus causing further suffering. After talking with the patient's physicians, the guardian suggested that the doctors refrain from further treatment and told the court: "Not treating Mr. Saikewicz would be in his best interest."[70] The court agreed, and further treatment was suspended.

The Hospice Movement

As more people considered such incidents and the overtreatment of some terminally ill individuals, a grassroots movement began that changed how terminally ill patients were treated. Author William H. Colby elaborates, "Modern hospice began as a grassroots movement in the 1970s, growing originally from the dissatisfaction of the families and some caregivers of cancer patients with their care and dying."[71] Hospice care often begins where traditional treatment ends: when it becomes apparent that a patient will not survive his or her illness. Whether the patient has one week or several months to live, hospice professionals work with the patient and family to make those last months pain free.

"AN UNDERLYING NEED"

"There is considerable evidence which suggests that a request for assistance in suicide may mask an underlying need for pain relief."
—Legal and medical journalist Philip King.

Philip King, "*Washington v. Glucksberg:* Influence of the Court in the Care of the Terminally Ill and Physician-Assisted Suicide," *Journal of Law and Health*, June 22, 2000.

The word *hospice* comes from the Latin word *hospis*, which means "host." In the Middle Ages, tired and sick travelers who were returning from the Crusades were often given shelter along the way in hospice houses that had been set up by the church. Since that time, the word has taken on a slightly different meaning. Hospice care is also called palliative care, meaning that treatment is focused on relief of symptoms only. Journalist King

Dame Cicely Saunders (left) began the modern hospice movement. Here she receives her doctorate degree from Dr. Donald Coggan, the archbishop of Canterbury.

explains, "The goal of palliative care is to relieve suffering and place the utmost importance on the quality of the patient's life."[72] It focuses on the process of dying, rather than the prevention of death. Hospice physician David Cundiff further elaborates, "With excellent palliative care, the dying process can . . . be associated with profound emotional and spiritual growth for the patients, as well as for the loved ones and caregivers."[73] As such, hospice care is widely accepted by both the medical profession and the public.

While a hospice was once associated with a building, today, according to former hospice director Linda Koeppen, "hospice . . . refers not to a place but rather to a program of care, based on a philosophy that recognizes dying as part of the normal process of living and focuses on enhancing the quality of remaining life."[74] Hospice organizations stress that their care affirms life, including the need for patients to be given all the necessary and available

Dame Cicely Saunders

Cicely Saunders was the founder of Great Britain's first modern hospice and is credited with being the first modern doctor to devote his or her practice to the care of the dying. Saunders began work as a registered nurse during World War II, but a back problem led her to pursue a career in social work. In the course of her work, she helped care for a dying Polish patient named David Tasma. Together, the two of them conceived an idea for a place where the dying could be properly treated. Using a sum of money left her by Tasma, Saunders began to work on the idea.

Doctors who worked at the hospital where Saunders was assigned were supportive but suggested she might have better luck if she, herself, were a physician. At age thirty-three, she enrolled in medical school and eventually qualified as a physician. She was given a research scholarship to study pain management in the terminally ill and gained important experience in caring for terminally ill patients.

She put her expertise to work when she opened St. Christopher's Hospice. The hospice was put on the national registry as a charity in 1961. The first patient was admitted in 1967, and by 1970 Great Britain's National Health Service was providing two-thirds of the cost for operation. By providing excellent pain control and a home-like environment, Saunders revolutionized the care of the terminally ill.

The news of her hospice spread throughout the world. Hospices based on her concept now exist in North America and throughout the English-speaking world.

support during the process of dying. Hospice physician Cundiff summarizes, "Hospice seeks to optimize the quality of life."[75]

The modern hospice movement was begun by English physician Cicely Saunders in 1967 when she opened St. Christopher's Hospice in Great Britain. Saunders, while working in other hospitals, had been shocked by the treatment received by dying patients and the emotional and physical suffering that most patients endured.

Hospice came to America in the 1970s. One of Cicely Saunders's nurses was Florence Wald, later the dean of Yale University Nursing School. In 1974 Wald helped open the first hospice in the United States—Connecticut Hospice in Branford. That same year the National Cancer Institute began providing funds to all hospices in the United States, and in the mid-1980s Medicare and Medicaid joined other insurance companies in covering hospice care. As a rule, this coverage takes care of providing medication, equipment, and care for the terminally ill.

In 1993, 11 percent of U.S. deaths occurred in hospices; by 2004 that number had risen to 31 percent. Currently, 450,000 patients die each year while under hospice care provided by over three thousand American hospices. This represents about 20 percent of all deaths, which number around 2.5 million annually. Writer Colby summarizes, "Hospice today is a major health care field with extensive government regulation."[76]

There are two basic kinds of hospice care. The most common is home care, where nurses and other health care professionals visit patients in their homes and provide support to the caregivers, who are often family members. When home care becomes impossible because of caregiver fatigue or unrelieved pain or other symptoms, the patient is often brought to an inpatient facility. These facilities have eased the burden for nonprofessional caregivers and offer twenty-four-hour care by nurses and other professionals.

The Issue of Pain and Suffering

Hospice care also offers an alternative way for dying patients to end their lives. Rather than resorting to suicide or assisted suicide or enduring the dying process in an institutionalized setting, patients and their families can choose hospice care. Joe Loconte, in an article titled "Hospice, Not Hemlock" written in 1998, opined, "Hospice care is an important option for patients who do not wish to die a depersonalized death in a hospital or attempt assisted suicide."[77] Loconte's opinion is one that is shared by the majority of hospice professionals.

Hospice experts cite that the main reason it is such a good alternative is that hospice care provides good pain control and an end to needless suffering. Psychiatrist and best-selling author M. Scott Peck elaborates, "Nothing fuels the euthanasia debate so much as the fear of intractable physical pain."[78] Peck, like many medical personnel, believes the answer lies not in euthanasia but in better pain management. "Until such improvement occurs," Peck concludes, "the issue of physical suffering will remain a factor in the euthanasia debate."[79]

One of the first problems that hospices tackled, in fact, was pain control. Acute, short-term pain is viewed as a signal that something is wrong. This kind of pain usually results from a disease process or injury that can be readily treated and resolved within a relatively short period of time.

The pain associated with terminal cancer is far different. Author Cundiff explains: "The pain of cancer is particularly meaningless, serving no useful purpose such as warning the sufferer of imminent harm. . . . Cancer pain usually grows more rather than less severe."[80] In addition to the physical agony that severe pain can cause, it also has other components. These include psychological pain, fear, anxiety, and spiritual pain from a life that suddenly seems to have no meaning.

A CONSTITUTIONAL RIGHT

"From a legal standpoint, patients in the United States have a constitutionally recognized right to refuse any and all forms of medical intervention, whether or not they are terminal and whether or not such refusal may lead to their death." —Medical journalists Paul S. Mueller and C. Christopher Hook.

Paul S. Mueller and C. Christopher Hook, "The Terri Schiavo Saga: The Making of a Tragedy and Lessons Learned," *Mayo Clinic Proceedings,* November 1, 2005.

Prior to the development of hospices, pain control of the terminally ill, as well as cancer patients in general, was sadly ineffectual. Said one patient: "They used to see how long I could go without an injection. I used to be pouring with sweat because of the pain. I couldn't speak to anyone and I was having crying fits."[81] The same patient, hospitalized in a hospice, reported to his hospice caregivers much better pain control.

Hospice professionals believe that pain control is one of the most important issues for the dying patient. From the beginning of the hospice movement, the alleviation of pain was addressed. Within a short time, pain ceased to be a problem for the majority of hospice patients. The reason for the improvement was the

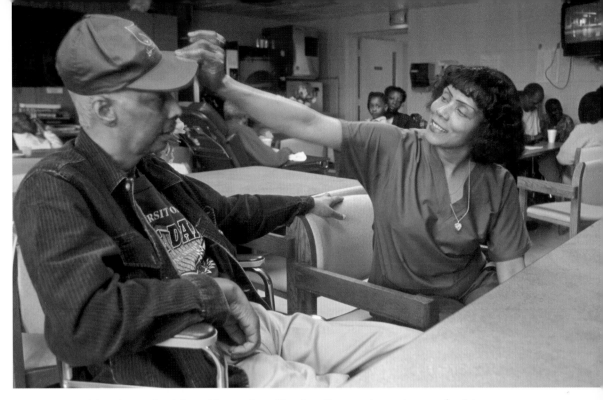

A hospice worker jokes with a patient. Hospice offers an alternative way for dying patients to end their lives.

use of continuous doses of medication, rather than waiting for the patient to ask for them. The hospice philosophy contends that constant pain needs constant pain control. This aggressive use of opiates has become the standard for all hospice care. Author James Haley summarizes, "Once the pain and symptoms of an illness are under control, people rarely talk about taking their own lives."[82] This argument is made not only by hospice professionals but many right-to-life advocates as well.

Pain control is now part of many specialty areas of medicine, and many medical schools now offer courses to help physicians understand the reasoning behind aggressive use of narcotics in patients with cancer. Many medical associations, explains journalist King, advocate that it is "morally appropriate to increase the dosage to levels needed even to the point where death is hastened, provided that the primary objective of the necessary treatment plan is to relieve pain."[83]

Hospice makes the argument that assisted suicide is thus unnecessary. Registered nurse Rosemary Ferdinand elaborates, "In nearly all patients, they say, pain and other symptoms can be relieved if they are carefully assessed and treated."[84] Hospice physician David Cundiff agrees: "In my view, improved care of the terminally ill will make the question of euthanasia and assisted suicide moot."[85]

Refusal of Treatment on Religious Grounds

The passive euthanasia that is practiced by hospice in its support of refusing aggressive treatment is widely accepted by nearly all physicians and the public. The passive euthanasia practiced by various religious groups that involves the refusal of medical treatment is not so acceptable to the medical profession and much of the public. Critics contend that members of the religious communities are not terminally ill. Instead the members have readily treatable illnesses that sometimes become fatal because of nontreatment.

The refusal of medical care, particularly in the case of children, by some religions has become, in many eyes, a conflict and a source of grave concern in American society. Critics of this practice argue that hospice patients die from the disease, not from the refusal of treatment. However, the children of these religious groups die not so much from the disease, but from the lack of medical treatment. While the refusal of treatment by adults is often considered ill-advised, the nontreatment of children is considered tragic. Even those who support the most basic tenets of an individual's right to die consider such deaths as violating a child's right to live.

Critics of the refusal of treatment on medical grounds point most often to the practitioners of Christian Science. Journalist Larry May explains, "Since the Christian Science Church was founded over a century ago by Mary Baker Eddy, Christian Scientists have been locked in a struggle with the medical profession."[86]

Christian Scientists believe that each person should be his or her own physician. In addition, they believe that all illness has an emotional component. The Christian Science Church explains: "Christian Science teaches that all problems . . . have a mental basis. . . . Therefore, a quick solution through medicine would not address the real issue, since such a treatment doesn't deal with the mental aspect of the condition."[87]

Most physicians disagree, claiming that it is a violation of their professional duties and oath to "do not harm" to allow suffering that could be prevented by medical treatment. Christian Scientists, however, claim that it contravenes their religious freedom to be forced to subject their children to medical treatment in violation of their religious beliefs. Furthermore, the Christian Science Church has frequently claimed that its method of healing through the use prayer is as effective or superior to medicine in healing all childhood illness. Heather Hayward, a Christian Science practitioner, explains: "I've faced some severe physical situations of my own . . . but my instinctive reaction, based on previous experiences of spiritual healing, has been to always

The Christian Science Church's reliance on faith healing, as shown in this carving on the stone exterior of the church's London headquarters, has resulted in some battles over a practitioner's right to refuse medical treatment.

trust God for the resolution."[88] This has led to heated arguments between physicians and practitioners of the religion.

Incidents Fuel the Fire

While the judicial system has upheld the right of members of religious groups to refuse treatment for themselves and their children, critics of the practice cite numerous examples of children who could have been saved from death by modern medical treatment. These incidents fuel the fire of opposition to allowing such religious groups to refuse treatment. Religious groups are protected by a federal law enacted in 1974 as an addendum to the Child Abuse and Treatment Act that states, "A parent or guardian who does not provide medical treatment to a child because of the parent's religious beliefs is not considered, for that reason alone, to be a negligent parent or guardian."[89]

One state group, Massachusetts Citizens for Children, a grassroots, nonpartisan, nonprofit group whose goal is to prevent child abuse through electoral and legislative action, asserts, "Unfortunately there is a tragic public record of Christian Science's failure to save children from a number of normal non-fatal illnesses."[90] The group points specifically to two children in the late 1980s who died of juvenile diabetes, a childhood illness that is normally nonfatal when treated with medication. The children received no medical treatment, only prayer.

These cases were not isolated incidents. In April 1986 one child, Robyn Twitchell, ate dinner and then experienced severe pain and vomiting. His symptoms continued for two days, during which he was treated by Christian Science health practitioners with prayer. Five days after the initial attack, the child died. An autopsy showed that Robyn had a bowel obstruction, something that could have been corrected with surgery and hospital treatment. Robyn's case did not involve diabetes, but critics of Christian Science healing used it to illustrate that, in many cases, simple hospital treatment by skilled medical professionals could save the lives of many children within the Christian Science faith.

Such cases shock the general public and anger medical practitioners. Members of the public, especially those who are parents, are sickened by stories of an innocent child losing his or her life due to what they perceive as neglect for failure to pursue medical treatment. Author Larry May elaborates, "It seems clear to most physicians that respecting the beliefs and choices of Christian Scientists meant that Robyn's right to life and his right to minimally adequate health care were jeopardized."[91] The American medical establishment has long been critical of and opposed to the refusal of medical care by religious groups.

The Christian Science religion counters these arguments with stories of the many people who have been cured by religious

The Pennsylvania Hospital in Philadelphia has offered "bloodless" surgery to Jehovah's Witnesses for years. Jehovah's Witnesses believe that the Bible forbids blood transfusions.

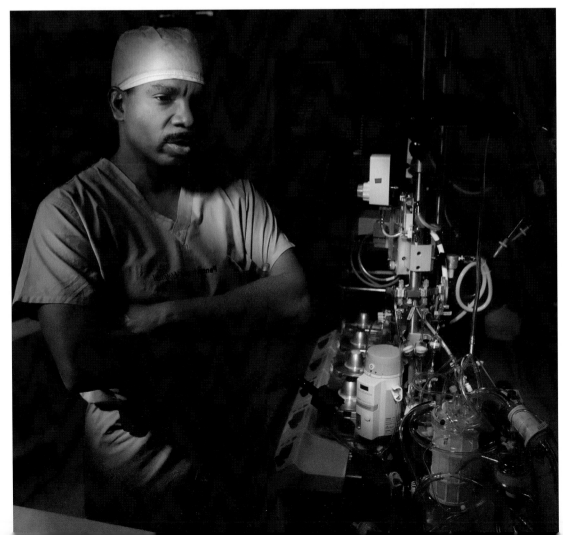

healing and faith. Virginia S. Harris, former chair of the Christian Science Board of Directors, relates the story of one such healing that she was involved in: "When I first met a girl called Linda, she was fourteen years old. She suffered from what her doctors had diagnosed as arterial venous malformation [a congenital condition in which a person's veins and arteries do not connect in the proper manner]. She'd had piercing head pains since childhood and had missed a lot of school." Her doctors had given a dire prognosis: She would suffer pain her entire life unless she had surgery that offered only a 50 percent chance of survival. Harris intervened at the mother's request and met with Linda for several weeks, offering prayer and counseling. At the end of four weeks, Linda was off her medication; at the end of two months she was healed. Harris continues: "That was eighteen years ago. Today she's married and has two children."[92]

DRAWING A LINE

"[Many feel that a line] needs to be drawn at the point where respecting a religious minority culture clearly jeopardizes the well-being of children." —Ethicist Larry May.

Larry May, "Challenging Medical Authority: The Refusal of Treatment by Christian Scientists," *Hastings Center Report*, January 1, 1995.

The Jehovah's Witness religion also views some medical intervention as contrary to its religious beliefs. This is particularly evident in members' refusal to allow blood transfusions. They point to the Bible as their reason for this abstention and cite Acts 15:29: "keep abstaining from . . . blood." Other than blood products, Jehovah's Witnesses, however, allow medical treatment when appropriate, due to their nonbelief in faith healing. Like Christian Scientists, these religious followers have been criticized by the medical profession when a child or adult dies when a blood transfusion may have prevented the death.

The American Academy of Pediatrics has led a campaign to remove the religious exemptions to child neglect and endangerment statutes. This group is fueled, writes May, by the "belief that

Christian Scientists and Jehovah's Witnesses should be forced to subject their children to the full range of curative powers at the disposal of modern medicine. . . . The religious exemption is seen as a major impediment to providing the best health care to all American children."[93]

Massachusetts Citizens for Children is also very vocal in its opposition to the laws that protect religious groups. It states:

> The state cannot regulate religious healing. It cannot set standards for the training of faith healers or certify their credentials to take life and death responsibility for help-less children . . . the Christian Science Church has presented no scientifically credible evidence that its methods can heal serious childhood illness. . . . Christian Science parents should not be exempted from the legal responsibility of all other Massachusetts parents to provide their seriously ill children with necessary medical care.[94]

Christian Science practitioners counter this argument by claiming that it would be hypocritical for their followers to rely on mainstream medicine when they have faith in the power of prayer.

THE WITHDRAWAL OF LIFE-SUSTAINING TREATMENT

People who are terminally ill can consciously decide whether to continue or stop treatment. They are also able to choose whether to live out their remaining days with hospice care or to enlist the assistance of a physician to hasten their death. Likewise, members of certain religious communities are able to make conscious decisions about accepting or refusing potentially life-saving medical treatment. For some individuals, however, making such decisions for themselves is impossible.

The problem derives from the fact that in this modern age of medicine, patients can be kept alive, even though they are no longer conscious or have any chance of recovery. Life-prolonging treatment covers a span of many different options, including medication such as antibiotics, blood transfusions, respirators, artificial nutrition and hydration, and dialysis. With these kinds of treatments available, patients can be kept alive for an almost indefinite period of time. In these situations, the question then becomes whether keeping a patient with no hope of recovery alive is more detrimental to the person than not keeping them alive. Writer George Burnell asks the pertinent question: "Are we prolonging the dying or prolonging the living?"[95]

While opposing the use of assisted suicide, many major religions and other groups have agreed that withdrawing life-sustaining treatment for those who have no hope of recovery is an acceptable option. And yet, many others argue that even patients who are at death's door should not have that life shortened by the withdrawal of treatment. They argue that life is sacred at every stage and should be prolonged until a natural death occurs.

Many doctors, as a result of this conflict, worry that they may be charged with malpractice or even wrongful killing if they stop potentially life-sustaining treatment. Physicians are so concerned about the possibility that they will be charged with murder that they often continue treatment, sometimes in defiance of the patient's and family's wishes.

Persistent Vegetative State

The controversy over withdrawing medical treatment came about because of a new medical condition. This new diagnosis was necessary because of the improvement in medical technology. Before the 1970s, when a patient experienced a cardiac arrest or cessation of heart function, they were simply declared dead. With the invention of cardiopulmonary resuscitation

Dialysis treatment prolongs the lives of patients with kidney failure.

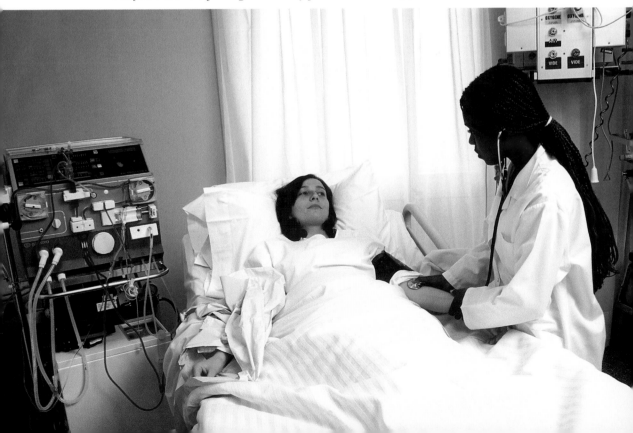

(CPR), oftentimes patients who experienced a cardiac arrest were revived and placed on life-sustaining machines such as artificial respirators. In many cases, however, the patients had been without oxygen for an extended period of time, and their brains had suffered massive damage. What looked like a coma persisted for many months with no signs of improvement and was named a persistent vegetative state.

The term "persistent vegetative state" came into use for the first time in 1972. A coma or sleep-like state is usually limited in its duration, while a vegetative state is unlimited and usually persists until the death of the patient occurs. Patients in a vegetative state appear to be awake at times but are totally unaware of their surroundings. Their eyes may move around the room, and they might smile or make noises, but these actions are purely reflex and not indicative of any level of consciousness. Writers Paul W. Armstrong and B.D. Cohen elaborate: "They cannot, and will not ever again, be able to see, hear, speak, respond, think, or feel on even the most rudimentary level."[96]

FIGHTING FOR THE DEFENSELESS

"We must work diligently to not only help Terri Schiavo continue her own fight for life, but to join the fight of all those who have lost the capacity to fight on their own." —Representative James Sensenbrenner, commenting on government intervention.

Quoted in Neal Conan, "Analysis: Terri Schiavo Case and End-of-Life Decisions," NPR, *Talk of the Nation*, March 21, 2005.

Problems immediately arose in these patients, who had such massive brain damage that there was no hope of recovery. In many cases, the patients were young and had suffered the injuries after an automobile accident or other catastrophic event. Families were torn apart with the need to make decisions about stopping treatment of their loved ones. The decisions were made more difficult by the age of many of the patients and the lack of any guidelines or laws that dealt with such situations. In addition, most young patients lack advance directives such as a living will or medical power of attorney. These documents clearly outline what treatment a person wants and does not want.

Surrogate Decision-Makers

In the absence of any advance directives, physicians are faced with the dilemma of approaching a family member about treatment. Some states have enacted laws that clearly define the order of preference in a family having to make decisions for a comatose patient. *New York Times* journalist Shaila Dwan elaborated in

Advance Directives

Many medical experts believe that the use of advance directives could potentially end the conflict surrounding the withdrawal of life-sustaining treatment. In 1969 human rights lawyer Luis Kutner proposed a new document to help patients retain control over those decisions: a living will. California was the first state to adopt his suggestion, but other states soon followed. In addition to the living will, many states also authorize the use of a durable power of attorney for health care. Together, the two documents are called advance directives.

A living will is a document that specifies the circumstances under which a person might not want continued medical care. A durable power of attorney names a surrogate, usually a family member, to make such decisions when a person is no longer able to do so. These documents are recognized in most states but are underused. Less than 25 percent

of Americans, for instance, have made out a living will.

Editor James Haley has provided a sample of the California Advance Health Care Directive: "I do not want efforts made to prolong my life and I do not want life-sustaining treatment to be provided or continue: (1) if I am in an irreversible coma or persistent vegetative state; or (2) if I am terminally ill and the application of life-sustaining procedures would serve only to artificially delay the moment of my death."

Despite the benefits of these documents, they still have many drawbacks. Unfortunately, many hospitals and physicians ignore them or do not know about them. In addition, the living will tends to be limited in scope and practice; it cannot predict or dictate treatment in every possible condition.

Quoted in James Haley, ed., *Opposing Viewpoints: Death and Dying.* Farmington Hills, MI: Greenhaven, 2003, p. 60.

October 2003: "Overwhelmingly, state laws and courts have granted the spouse the first right to make life-or-death decisions. . . . This reflects the view that spouses are better equipped to make proxy decisions because they share responsibilities and have known each other intimately in their adult lives, rather than in childhood."[97]

Eventually, the court system came up with an answer in the form of surrogate decision-makers and the concept of substituted judgment. Colby explains: "Using this concept, a substi-

Difficult end-of-life decisions often fall to surrogate decision-makers.

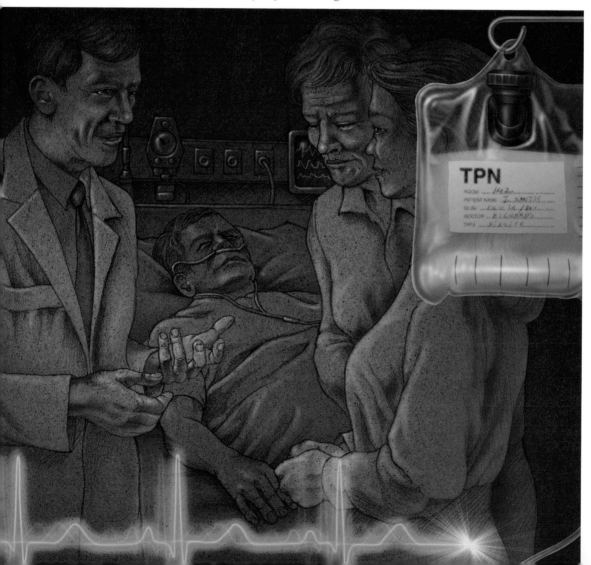

tute decision-maker exercises the right of the incapacitated person by trying to determine what the person would want."[98] In some cases, the court actually assumes this role.

A surrogate decision-maker has many legal obligations. He or she is required to follow a patient's advance directives and, in the absence of such documents, must use what the court refers to as substituted judgment. Medical journalists Paul S. Mueller and C. Christopher Hook explain this concept: "Knowing the worldview, values, goals, and fears of the patient and making decisions as closely as possible to those the patient would make if capable."[99]

The 1983 President's Commission for the Study of Ethical Problems in Medicine further addressed this issue and concluded: "When making decisions about medical treatment for a seriously ill loved one, the decision-maker must take into account such factors as the relief of suffering, the preservation or restoration of functioning, and the quality as well as the extent of life sustained."[100]

Doctors, however, are often in dispute with such surrogate decision-makers. Writer Burnell explains, "More often than not, doctors feel compelled to continue treatment once they have started it . . . even if it is futile in improving the patient's condition."[101] In addition, physicians are bound by their medical oaths to act as their patients' advocates. If, for instance, they believe that the surrogate is not acting in the best interests of the patient, they can challenge any decision that might work to their patients' disadvantage. Many physicians and hospital administrators have used this principle and have asked the court to appoint an alternative decision-maker.

Many moral and ethical issues arose in the care of patients in a persistent vegetative state. Three major cases over a thirty-year period have helped shape public opinion about patients in a persistent vegetative state. And yet, to date, the issue of withdrawing life-sustaining treatment remains unsolved as each state wrestles with its own definitions and policies.

Karen Ann Quinlan

The first case that gained public recognition was that of Karen Ann Quinlan, a twenty-one-year-old woman. On the night of

Karen Ann Quinlan was ruled to be in a persistent vegetative state, but her family had to fight a court battle with the hospital administrators to remove her artificial respirator in 1976.

April 15, 1975, she went to a local tavern in Landing, New Jersey, with friends. While there, she had several alcoholic beverages and then began to act oddly. Unknown to all concerned, Quinlan had also taken sedatives, or barbiturates, prior to her evening on the town. Her friends took her home and put her in bed, but when they checked on her hours later, she was not breathing. One of her friends started mouth-to-mouth resuscitation and called for an ambulance. Quinlan eventually started breathing on her own again but never regained consciousness. When she arrived at the emergency room, her pupils did not react to light, nor did she respond to pain. Both were physical signs of massive brain damage caused by the lack of oxygen. She was placed on an artificial respirator to help her breathe, and her parents were notified. She was eventually diagnosed as being in a persistent vegetative state.

After consulting with their priest, attorney, and other family members, the Quinlans asked the physicians to remove the artificial respirator and allow their daughter to die naturally. The hospital administrator advised Quinlan's physicians not to comply with the parents' wishes. The Quinlans then took the case to court, where a judge ordered the removal of the respirator. Still, the hospital refused to take action. Julia Quinlan, Karen's mother, explained the family's feelings: "We didn't ask for Karen to die. We just asked for her to be removed from technology and be placed in a natural state."[102]

Her physicians, however, were afraid that if they removed her respirator, they would be guilty of murder. In addition,

Ralph Porzoi, the hospital's attorney, argued: "If Karen Ann Quinlan has one chance in a thousand, if she has one chance in ten thousand, if she has one chance in a million, who are we and by what right do we kill that chance? Who are we and by what right do we kill that life?"[103]

Withdrawing Treatment in Infants

The withholding of treatment for infants with disabilities and other problems has long been a controversial issue. As smaller and smaller premature infants began to survive, the issue intensified. The death of one baby in the 1980s brought nationwide attention to the problem.

Baby Doe was born in April 1982 in Bloomington, Indiana, with Down syndrome and esophageal atresia. The infant's esophagus was not connected to his stomach, meaning the child could not swallow or absorb food. Doctors recommended surgery and a temporary feeding tube to repair the problem. The parents refused, in part because of the Down syndrome, but also because surgeons offered less than a 50 percent chance of improvement. The parents also refused a permanent feeding tube and intravenous therapy. Hospital officials immediately went to court, demanding treatment for the infant. County prosecutors filed an emergency petition asking the court to take custody of the child. Before the issue could be resolved in the courts, Baby Doe died. Criticism of the parents began almost immediately. Pointing out that the baby was not comatose, a *Wash-ington Post* editorial weighed in: "The Indiana baby died not because he couldn't sustain life without a million dollars worth of medical machinery but because no one fed him." Proponents of the right to life considered the incident an infanticide—the murder of an innocent newborn.

This case and others compelled then president Ronald Reagan to take action to prevent similar situations. On October 9, 1984, Reagan signed the Child Abuse Amendments of 1984, making it illegal for doctors to withhold nourishment or other medically indicated treatments unless an infant was comatose. The act specified that treatment was indicated unless "(1) the infant was irreversibly comatose; (2) if treatment would merely prolong dying; or (3) if the treatment would be virtually futile in terms of the survival of the infant and the treatment itself under such circumstances would be inhumane."

Quoted in Peter G. Filene, *In the Arms of Others: A Cultural History of the Right to Die in America.* Chicago: Ivan R. Dee, 1998, p. 108.

Quoted in Meiling Rein, Abbey M. Begun, and Jacquelyn F. Quiram, *Death and Dying: Who Decides?* Wylie, TX: Information Plus, 1998, p. 56.

A court battle ensued that finally reached the New Jersey Supreme Court. On March 31, 1976, the court handed down a decision in *Re Quinlan*, finding that Quinlan's right to privacy should include her right to be removed from the respirator. Chief Justice Richard Hughes spoke for the court: "We have no hesitancy in deciding . . . that no external compelling interest of the state could compel Karen to endure the unendurable . . . with no realistic possibility of returning to any semblance of cognitive . . . life."[104] The court further ruled that Quinlan's parents could use their best judgment in removing the respirator. The respirator was finally removed, but Quinlan did not die. She would linger another ten years before finally succumbing on June 11, 1985.

Do Not Harm

"To demand that we impose unwanted treatments on a patient for whom there is no prospect of improvement, who has left verbal information expressing his or her life and health care values and goals but did not take the time to or could not complete an advance directive, is unconscionable and violates the oldest of ethical principles—nonmaleficence or do not harm." —Paul S. Mueller and C. Christopher Hook.

Paul S. Mueller and C. Christopher Hook, "The Terri Schiavo Saga: The Making of a Tragedy and Lessons Learned," *Mayo Clinic Proceedings*, November 1, 2005.

In the wake of the Quinlan case, several notable things occurred. The U.S. Congress passed a law in 1978 that established a presidential commission to study ethical problems in medicine and biomedical research. Even more importantly, many hospitals throughout the United States formed ethics committees. These committees were charged with arbitrating issues between patients and their families and their doctors.

Artificial Feeding

Quinlan's lingering death after the respirator was removed brought up another highly controversial and emotional issue—the use of artificial feeding methods to sustain life. Modern med-

Water bottles are left in the Piazza del Duomo in Milan, Italy, in protest of a court order to stop the feeding and hydration of a woman in an irreversible coma.

icine has developed a method of surgically inserting a feeding tube directly into the stomach, which can be used long-term in feeding and hydrating patients. Armstrong and Cohen explain why this is important: "Further complicating the issue, is the fact that many persistent vegetative state patients survive for long periods of time without mechanical ventilation. Thus the question with these patients is whether the continuation of artificial nutrition and hydration is medically indicated."[105] Many pro-life supporters base their support on the presumption that even patients who would not want extraordinary life-sustaining measures would want basic hydration and nutrition.

The issue of hydration is thus fraught with emotional and psychological importance. Author Burnell explains: "Most people perceive food and water as a basic sign of nurturance and a minimum commitment to the well-being of another person."[106] This emotionalism revolves around the issue of the starving patient. Many right-to-life groups have focused on the belief that withdrawing nutrition and hydration will cause a painful and horrible death. St. Louis neurologist William Burke states: "A conscious person . . . will go into seizures. Their skin cracks, their tongues crack, their lips crack. . . . Death by dehydration takes ten to fourteen days. It is an extremely agonizing death."[107] Many other physicians argue that this is simply not true, claiming that as the muscle and tissue break down, the patient is generally too weak to feel thirst or hunger. They claim that, generally, such deaths are peaceful and quiet, with the patient slipping into an unconscious state and feeling no discomfort as death approaches.

Nancy Cruzan

The hydration and artificial nutrition of a patient was challenged in the 1980s by the parents of Nancy Cruzan, a twenty-six-year-old woman who was involved in an automobile accident in 1983.

Nancy Cruzan was at the center of a court battle to stop the artificial feeding and hydration that kept her alive following a car accident that left her in a coma.

Thrown from the car, Cruzan was found by paramedics lying face down in a water-filled ditch. Finding no heartbeat and no respirations, the medics began cardiopulmonary resuscitation and removed her to the nearest hospital. Emergency room physicians found her comatose but breathing on her own and admitted her to the hospital. After lingering in a coma for many months, her physicians diagnosed Cruzan as a persistent vegetative state patient with no possibility of recovery or improvement.

QUALITY OF LIFE

"Engaging in life is the key to my assessment of my own quality of life. . . . If all medicine can do is sustain me in a vegetative state . . . without hope of living life again, then I believe the medicine or technology should be stopped, and earlier rather than later."
—Lawyer William H. Colby, attorney for Nancy Cruzan's family.

William H. Colby, *Unplugged: Reclaiming Our Right to Die in America.* New York: AMACOM, 2006, p. 130.

In the meantime, doctors had inserted a feeding tube to provide nutrition and hydration. Cruzan's parents, after long deliberation, eventually asked the doctors to remove the feeding tube and allow their daughter to die naturally. The hospital refused to comply with their request, leading to a number of court cases as the Cruzans fought for their daughter's right to die.

The case drew nationwide attention. For the first time, television viewers saw a patient in a persistent vegetative state and were kept informed about her parent's struggle. Public opinion polls in 1990 showed overwhelming support for the Cruzans: 88 percent of Missourians and 90 percent of Missouri physicians agreed that it was right to remove the tube.

After long deliberation and many court appearances, the Cruzan case was finally heard by the U.S. Supreme Court in *Cruzan v. Missouri.* The Court ruled for the state of Missouri, saying that the state had not violated the Constitution in denying the removal of the feeding tube. Chief Justice William Rehnquist, on July 25, 1990, however, did leave the door open for a new trial should any new evidence of Cruzan's actual wishes come to light. Three of her friends ultimately came forward and testified about several conversations they had had with Cruzan, during which she had indicated her desire for no life support. With this new evidence in hand, the Cruzans appealed the decision. This time, the Missouri attorney general chose not to oppose the family. The feeding tube was removed, and Nancy Cruzan eventually died a natural death in December 1990.

POLITICAL VERSUS PRIVATE MATTERS

"Do we really want to set the precedent of this great body, the United States Congress, to insert ourselves in the middle of families' private matters all across America?" —Representative Debbie Wasserman Schultz, commenting on government intervention.

Quoted in Neal Conan, "Analysis: Terri Schiavo Case and End-of-Life Decisions," NPR, *Talk of the Nation*, March 21, 2005.

Author Cox summarizes: "Nancy's death intensified the intensive and bitter national debate between those who believe that people should be allowed to die with dignity and others who have argued that even life in a vegetative state has a meaning."[108] There was no easy answer, and it would be left to later courts to make their own determinations.

Continued Debate

Despite the various court rulings, the problems surrounding the removal of a feeding tube arose again in New Jersey when the parents of Nancy Ellen Jobes filed for the right to remove their daughter's artificial nutrition. The issue was nearly identical to that of Cruzan. Authors Armstrong and Cohen explain: "Physicians and health care facility administrators were refusing to allow the withdrawal of life-supporting technology from a patient for whom the treatment offered no hope of improvement —to say nothing of recovery."[109] Ultimately, the court ruled in Jobes's favor, enabling the family to have the feeding tube removed.

Despite this decree, other cases also went to court to settle the same basic questions: When can life-sustaining treatment be withdrawn? Do the patient and the family have the right to make these decisions? In Clearwater, Florida, for example, eighty-five-year-old Estelle Browning clearly specified in her living will that she did not wish to be kept alive by means of an artificial feeding tube. Despite her wishes, she died with a feeding tube after a stroke rendered her unable to voice her wishes.

Another case in Florida had a different ending. Abe Perlmutter was a seventy-three-year-old man with Lou Gehrig's disease, a debilitating disease during which the patient loses all muscle control, including swallowing and breathing. He requested that his physicians remove his respirator. Unwilling to comply with his wishes, the hospital took the case to court, where an appellate court ruled that the patient's wishes superseded those of the state. The court stated:

> Abe Perlmutter should be allowed to make his choice to die with dignity. . . . It is all very convenient to insist on continuing Mr. P's life so that there can be no question of foul play. . . . However, it is quite another matter to do so at the patient's sole expense and against his competent will. . . . Such a course of conduct invades the patient's constitutional right of privacy, removes his freedom of choice, and invades his right to self-determine.[110]

Terri Schiavo

As the debate continued over withdrawing life-sustaining treatment, another heart-wrenching case gained worldwide attention. Once again, the nation watched as a family fought in the courts to settle the end-of-life decision to withdraw tube feeding.

Terri Schiavo was twenty-seven years old in 1990 when she suffered a cardiac arrest at home. While paramedics were able to restart her heart, Schiavo never regained consciousness, although she did open her eyes. Eventually she was diagnosed with persistent vegetative disorder, given no hope of recovery, and discharged from the hospital to a variety of nursing homes and rehabilitation centers. Her husband, Michael, was immediately appointed Terri's legal guardian. Terri Schiavo's situation reached crisis stage in 1993.

Terri Schiavo's parents tried to keep the hospital from removing the feeding tube that kept her alive in a persistent vegetative state by claiming that she was not truly brain dead.

The crisis resulted from a strong difference of opinion about Terri's care between her husband and her parents, Mary and Bob Schindler. After consultations with various specialists, Michael sued the hospital to have Terri's feeding tube removed. He had been told by Terri's neurologist that his wife had, in fact, died in the first hours after her collapse and that there was absolutely no hope for recovery.

The Schindlers vehemently opposed this decision and fought to keep their daughter alive. They believed that their daughter was responding to them, smiling at them, following them around the room with her eyes, and trying to talk. They hired attorney David Gibbs to represent them in court. He met Terri in the hospital and described his experience: "I found Terri sitting in a recliner. . . . Absolutely nothing was hooked up to her [except the feeding tube]. No IV drip. No monitors. No ventilators. . . . It was clear that Terri understood who the different people were in the room. . . . At the sound of her mother's voice, Terri squealed with delight. . . . She was clearly animated and responsive, and very much alive."[111]

On May 11, 1998, Michael Schiavo filed a petition in probate court seeking authorization to remove all artificial life support, namely the feeding tube. Judge George Greer ruled on January 24, 2000, that the tube feedings could be stopped. The feedings stopped in April 2001 but, following a successful suit by the Schindlers, were restarted shortly thereafter. Other trials followed, and again Greer ruled on ceasing the life support, reordering the tube removed in October 2003.

The Government Steps In

In the meantime, however, the Schindlers had contacted Randall Terry, a strong right-to-life advocate. Right-to-life groups throughout the United States supported the Schindlers in their opposition to the feeding tube removal. The National Right to Life Organization stated: "Terri is not terminally ill. . . . To induce someone's death by denying him or her nutrition and hydration is an act of starvation."[112] Terry and other right-to-life supporters contended that not all persistent vegetative states were permanent, and they cited numerous examples of patients who had fully recovered after being in such a state for long periods of time.

Terry appealed on the Schindler's behalf to Governor Jeb Bush and the Florida legislature. On October 21, 2003, Terri's Law was passed, allowing the governor fifteen days to order the feeding tube reinserted in any patient without a living will. Schiavo's tube was consequently reinserted. David Gibbs, attorney for the Schindlers, later explained the law: "Our bill would have protected the disabled from having a feeding tube removed when there was a family disagreement regarding the disabled person's spoken end-of-life wishes."[113]

It was at this point that the Schiavo case reached the front page on newspapers around the world. The media began treating the Schiavo situation as a death watch, keeping viewers informed on a day-to-day basis of the latest news and the latest court case. Pictures of a debilitated yet smiling Terri covered the front pages of newspapers and appeared nightly on television.

Terri's Law was ultimately overturned and ruled unconstitutional on the grounds that the law was not in keeping with the separation of powers and that the executive and legislative branches of the Florida government could not overrule a decision of the judicial branch. The feeding tube was removed, per Judge Greer's order, on March 18, 2005. This decision, however, did not stop the Schindlers or federal legislators who were determined to protect what they perceived as Terri's right to life. Congressional leaders in both the Senate and the House of Representatives introduced bills to protect an incapacitated person's rights, namely a Bill for the Relief of the Parents of Theresa Marie Schiavo. After passage by both houses of Congress, President George W. Bush rushed to Washington from his vacation to sign the bill into law, calling for the reinsertion of the tube.

Following the passage of this law, the Schindlers filed an appeal with the U.S. District Court in Florida for the reinsertion of the tube. Judge James D. Whittemore issued a thirteen-page decision denying the Schindler's request. In his ruling, Whittemore wrote: "This court concludes that Theresa Schiavo's life and liberty interests were adequately protected by the extensive process provided in the state courts."[114] Furthermore, Whittemore ruled that the federal government lacked the jurisdiction to overturn a Florida court decision. Governor Bush, still not satisfied with the rulings, then ordered the Department of Children and Families to take custody of Terri so that the tube could be reinserted. Greer issued a restraining order to prevent this, which Bush observed, and Terri Schiavo died on March 31, 2005, ending the family's twelve-year struggle.

An autopsy showed, beyond a doubt, that Schiavo's brain was profoundly damaged. Florida's District Six medical examiner, Jon Thogmartin, reported, "The degree of brain damage Terri had sustained was severe and irreversible, and there was no hope of rehabilitation."[115] He also concluded that Terri was blind, thereby refuting the claims of the Schindlers that their daughter could see their movements.

Learning from Terri Schiavo

By the time Terri died, she had had her feeding tube removed and reinserted several times. In addition, there had been four-

Right to Life—Terri Schiavo

During the long battle between Michael Schiavo and the Schindlers, various groups made their feelings about the matter well known. Members of the right-to-life movement vehemently opposed the withdrawal of life-sustaining treatment for Schiavo. They spoke of the miracles that had occurred with such patients and specifically mentioned Carol Dusold, a young homecoming queen, who had been rendered comatose after a 1966 automobile accident. She spent four months in what physicians referred to as a persistent vegetative state. Her extremities drew up and contracted, and her weight dropped to 65 pounds, indicating a severely debilitated state with little hope of recovery. Physicians recommended the removal of life support, but Dusold's mother refused. Sometime later, Dusold revived and began a period of extensive rehabilitation. She eventually married and had a child, living with only a limp and slightly slurred speech.

The Schindler's attorney, David Gibbs, recounts another such story. In 1996 twenty-one-year-old Theresa de Vera lost consciousness and stopped breathing during a severe asthma attack. She ultimately settled into a deep coma that physicians diagnosed as a persistent vegetative state. Doctors told the family there was no hope of recovery, and yet four months later, she woke up. After rehabilitation, she relearned how to feed herself, speak, and use her upper body. She later graduated from college.

Right-to-life supporters cite many similar stories of people in lengthy comas regaining consciousness and, after rehabilitation, resuming a normal lifestyle. Some of those who have recovered contend that they were aware of everything going on around them, even conversations between family members and physicians.

teen different court appeals and numerous other motions and hearings in the Florida courts. In addition, five suits had been filed in Federal District Court, while the Supreme Court of the United States had ruled on four different occasions not to hear the case. In the end these cases settled nothing other than that Terri would be allowed to die.

Nor did Terri's death end the controversy surrounding the removal of life-sustaining treatment. The most critical voice came from the Schindler's attorney, David Gibbs, who stated, "Terri's case . . . set a dangerous precedent for all vulnerable Americans, especially those who are disabled, those who have terminal illnesses, those who can no longer speak for themselves, and perhaps one day even those who are indigent and unable to pay for costly health care."[116]

Many others believe that the Florida legislature, Governor Bush, the U.S. Congress, and President Bush had no business meddling in a private family matter. The majority of these critics believe that the case should never have gone to court in the first place. They stress that the removal of the feeding tube did not clash with the ethical guidelines of any medical or religious group. In fact, they argue, Florida law supported Michael Schiavo's right to have the tube removed, since he was her legal guard-

A man's shirt illustrates the number of days severely brain-damaged patient Terri Schiavo has gone without food and water after the court-ordered removal of her artificial feeding tube in March 2005.

ian. Editors of the *Orange County (CA) Register* wrote: "The Schiavo case has underscored the nation's deep distaste for what many regard as overbearing government intrusion, various polls show. 83% of respondents to a CBS News poll . . . said Congress and the president should stay out of such matters."[117]

WHAT WOULD TERRI WANT?

"I know that Terri doesn't want to be like this. Almost every time I saw Terri, I'd think how she'd hate being this way, how she'd never want to be this helpless, this dependent." —Michael Schiavo, Terri Schiavo's husband.

Michael Schiavo with Michael Hirsh, *Terri: The Truth*. New York: Dutton, 2006, p. 88.

Registered nurse Michele Mathes summarizes: "The case of Terri Schiavo was the most litigated medical case in history. It was the focus of legislatures and courts at both the state and federal level. Indeed, it spawned its own private law by Congress." Mathes then offers her opinion:

> For all that, though, can we say that Terri Schiavo was well served by the law? By the time she died, tens of thousands of words had been written about her life and death by attorneys, judges, journalists, advocates, pundits, health care professionals, ethicists, and ordinary folks. Most of it focused on determining . . . what Terri would have wanted in terms of end-of-life care. I believe it is safe to say that whatever Terri's choices would have been . . . she would not have wanted what actually happened.[118]

Need for Legislation

The tragedy that surrounded Terri Schiavo highlighted the need for legislation and guidelines that physicians, hospitals, and courts can use to ease the complicated nature of these kinds of cases. Legislatures are inconsistent and do not have clear rules on the issue. Instead most have a collection of court decisions and opinions, none of which provide a consistent standard for dealing with a patient in a persistent vegetative state.

Writers Armstrong and Cohen give their opinion:

> Beginning with the New Jersey Supreme Court in the Quinlan case, court after court, commission after commission, and even some legislators, have affirmed and reaffirmed the right of an incompetent patient—particularly those in a persistent vegetative state—through family members and guardians, to refuse life-sustaining medical treatment. Why then has it been necessary for [others] . . . to go through the same public hell endured . . . by the Quinlan family?[119]

"A DECISION TO END A LIFE"

"Make no mistake: Terri Schiavo was not terminally ill or near death. This case was not an end-of-life decision. This was a decision to end a life." —David Gibbs, attorney for Terri Schiavo's parents.

David Gibbs with Bob DeMoss, *Fighting for Dear Life*. Minneapolis, MN: Bethany House, 2006, p. 30.

Many of the questions surrounding the right-to-die issue remain unanswered. Assisted suicide, for instance, while legal in the state of Oregon, remains against the law elsewhere. Proponents of legalizing assisted suicide continue to petition legislatures for the passage of laws that would allow the terminally ill to end their own lives. At the same time, family members of those on life-support systems and those in a persistent vegetative state continue to struggle to deal with the difficult decisions of ending life-sustaining measures.

With medical costs rising annually, the cost of end-of-life care continues to rise, placing a burden on families, insurance companies, and the tax-paying public, who are helping offset medical costs. As the population continues to age, the issue of end-of-life care continues to be a concern. In the meantime, the controversy surrounding right-to-die issues continues unabated.

NOTES

Introduction: The Right to Die

1. George M. Burnell, *Final Choices: To Live or Die in an Age of Medical Technology*. New York: Insight, 1993, p. 32.
2. Quoted in Gerald A. Larue, *Playing God: Fifty Religions' Views on Your Right to Die*. Wakefield, RI: Moyer Bell, 1999, p. 159.
3. Ted Gest, "Is There a Right to Die? Now the Supreme Court May Decide If Care Can Be Halted," *U.S. News & World Report*, December 11, 1989, p. 35.
4. Donald W. Cox, *Hemlock's Cup: The Struggle for Death with Dignity*. Buffalo, NY: Prometheus, 1993, p. 222.
5. Cox, *Hemlock's Cup*, p. 19.

Chapter 1: Death and the Dying Process

6. Elisabeth Kübler-Ross, *On Death and Dying*. New York: Collier, 1969, p. 4.
7. John Cloud, "A Kinder, Gentler Death," *Time*, September 18, 2000, p. 60.
8. Burnell, *Final Choices*, p. 321.
9. James M. Hoefler and Brian E. Kamore, *Deathright: Culture, Medicine, Politics and the Right to Die*. Boulder, CO: Westview, 1994, p. 26.
10. Richard Venus, "When There's No Relief in Sight, Choosing Death Makes Sense," *Dayton Daily News*, November 12, 1998, p. 19A.
11. Quoted in Edd Doerr and M.L. Tina Stevens, "What Quinlan Can Tell Kevorkian About the Right to Die," *Humanist*, March 1, 1997, p. 10.

12. Quoted in Peter G. Filene, *In the Arms of Others: A Cultural History of the Right to Die in America*. Chicago: Ivan R. Dee, 1998, p. 63.

13. Charles F. McKhann, *A Time to Die: The Place for Physician Assistance*. New Haven, CT: Yale University Press, 1997, p. 2.

14. Hoefler and Kamore, *Deathright*, p. 43.

15. Pythia Peay, "A Good Death," *Common Boundary*, September/October 1997, p. 34.

16. Quoted in William H. Colby, *Unplugged: Reclaiming Our Right to Die in America*. New York: AMACOM, 2006, p. 75.

17. Doerr and Stevens, "What Quinlan Can Tell Kevorkian About the Right to Die," p. 10.

18. Quoted in James Haley, ed., *Death and Dying: Opposing Viewpoints*. Farmington Hills, MI: Greenhaven, 2003, p. 11.

19. Kübler-Ross, *On Death and Dying*, p. 7.

20. Quoted in *AP Worldstream*, "Elisabeth Kübler-Ross, Author of *On Death and Dying* and an Advocate for the Hospice Movement, Dies at 78," August 25, 2004. www.highbeam.com/doc/1P1-98364448.html.

21. Filene, *In the Arms of Others*, p. 71.

22. Hoefler and Kamore, *Deathright*, p. 123.

Chapter 2: Euthanasia

23. James D. Torr, ed., *Euthanasia: Opposing Viewpoints*. San Diego, CA: Greenhaven, 2000, p. 12.

24. Sylvia Diane Ledger, "Euthanasia and Assisted Suicide: There Is an Alternative," *Ethics and Medicine*, July 1, 2007.

25. Larue, *Playing God*, p. 36.

26. Quoted in Robert F. Weir, *Physician-Assisted Suicide*. Bloomington: Indiana University Press, 1997, p. 38.

27. Quoted in Weir, *Physician-Assisted Suicide*, p. 41.

28. M. Scott Peck, *Denial of the Soul: Spiritual and Medical Perspectives on Euthanasia and Mortality*. New York: Harmony, 1997, p. 113.

29. Michael S. Lief and H. Mitchell Caldwell, *And the Walls Came Tumbling Down*. New York: Scribner, 2004, p. 12.

30. McKhann, *A Time to Die*, p. 185.

31. Eric Marcus, *Why Suicide?* San Francisco: Harper, 1996, p. 169.

32. Edward J. Larson, "Euthanasia in America: Past, Present, and Future," *Michigan Law Review*, May 1, 2004, p. 1,245.

33. Derek Humphry, *Final Exit: The Practicalities of Self-Deliverance and Assisted Suicide for the Dying*. Eugene, OR: Hemlock Society, 1991, p. 17.

34. Quoted in Larue, *Playing God*, p. 80.

35. Quoted in Larue, *Playing God*, p. 206.

36. David Cundiff, *Euthanasia Is Not the Answer: A Hospice Physician's View*. Totowa, NJ: Humana, 1992, p. 69.

37. Quoted in Cundiff, *Euthanasia Is Not the Answer*, p. 68.

38. Hoefler and Kamore, *Deathright*, p. 161.

39. Quoted in McKhann, *A Time to Die*, p. 160.

40. Venus, "When There's No Relief in Sight, Choosing Death Makes Sense."

41. Quoted in Weir, *Physician-Assisted Suicide*, pp. 69–71.

42. Marcus, *Why Suicide?* p. 184.

Chapter 3: Assisted Suicide

43. Quoted in Tamara L. Roleff, ed., *Suicide: Opposing Viewpoints*. San Diego, CA: Greenhaven, 1998, p. 90.

44. Marcus, *Why Suicide?* p. 167.

45. Stephen Jamison, *Final Acts of Love: Families, Friends, and Assisted Dying*. New York: G.P. Putnam's Sons, 1995, p. 246.

46. Robert A. Walker, "Accepting Assisted Suicide First Step Down Slippery Slope," *Dayton Daily News*, November 12, 1998, p. 19A.

47. Ledger, "Euthanasia and Assisted Suicide."

48. Jamison, *Final Acts of Love*, p. 11.

49. Simonne Liberty, "Forcing the Dying to Go On Is Cruel," *Dayton Daily News*, November 13, 1998, p. 23A.

50. Roleff, *Suicide*, p. 88.

51. Jack Kevorkian, *Prescription: Medicide: The Goodness of a Planned Death*. Buffalo, NY: Prometheus, 1991, p. 192.

52. Quoted in Joni Eareckson Tada, *When Is It Right to Die?* Grand Rapids, MI: Zondervan, 1992, p. 38.

53. Quoted in Mike Wallace, "Dr. Jack Kevorkian Interview," CBS, *60 Minutes*, June 3, 2007.

54. Quoted in Colby, *Unplugged*, p. 190.

55. Quoted in Euthanasia—ProCon.org, "Should Dr. Kevorkian Be Considered a Criminal?" www.euthanasiaprocon.org/iskevorkiancriminal.html.

56. Quoted in PR Newswire, "Dr. Jack Kevorkian Released from Prison: Pledges to Obey Michigan's Assisted Suicide Law, Continue Advocacy for 'End of Life' Issues," June 5, 2007. www.highbeam.com/doc/1G1-164526336.html.

57. Quoted in Euthanasia—ProCon.org, "What Is the Oregon Death with Dignity Act?" www.euthanasiaprocon.org/oregonlaw.html.

58. Philip King, "*Washington v. Glucksberg:* Influence of the Court in Care of the Terminally Ill and Physician-Assisted Suicide," *Journal of Law and Health*, June 22, 2000, p. 271.

59. King, "*Washington v. Glucksberg.*"

60. McKhann, *A Time to Die*, p. 34.

61. Doerr and Stevens, "What Quinlan Can Tell Kevorkian About the Right to Die."

62. Quoted in Roleff, *Suicide*, p. 36.

63. Quoted in Ledger, "Euthanasia and Assisted Suicide."

64. Quoted in McKhann, *A Time to Die*, p. 215.

Chapter 4: Refusing Medical Treatment

65. Quoted in Weir, *Physician-Assisted Suicide*, p. 46.

66. Burnell, *Final Choices*, p. 95.

67. Cundiff, *Euthanasia Is Not the Answer*, p. 12.

68. Burnell, *Final Choices*, p. 106.

69. Quoted in Tada, *When Is It Right to Die?* p. 11.

70. Quoted in Filene, *In the Arms of Others*, p. 136.

71. Colby, *Unplugged*, p. 203.

72. King, *"Washington v. Glucksberg."*

73. Cundiff, *Euthanasia Is Not the Answer*, p. 15.

74. Linda Koeppen, "Hospice: Middle Ground Between End-of-Life Extremes," *Dayton Daily News*, November 12, 1998, p. 19A.

75. Cundiff, *Euthanasia Is Not the Answer*, p. 7.

76. Colby, *Unplugged*, p. 209.

77. Quoted in Haley, *Death and Dying*, p. 17.

78. Peck, *Denial of the Soul*, p. 27.

79. Peck, *Denial of the Soul*, p. 26.

80. Cundiff, *Euthanasia Is Not the Answer*, p. 106.

81. Quoted in Caroline Richmond, "Obituary: Dame Cicely Saunders: Founder of the Modern Hospice Movement," *Independent* (London), July 15, 2005, p. 38.

82. Haley, *Death and Dying*, p. 24.

83. King, *"Washington v. Glucksberg."*

84. Rosemary Ferdinand, "I'd Rather Die than Live This Way," *American Journal of Nursing*, December 1995, p. 42.

85. Cundiff, *Euthanasia Is Not the Answer*, p. viii.

86. Larry May, "Challenging Medical Authority: The Refusal of Treatment by Christian Scientists," *Hastings Center Report*, January 1, 1995, p. 15.

87. Christian Science, "About Christian Science: Your Questions and Answers." http://christianscience.com/blogs/questions-and-answers.

88. Quoted in Christian Science, "About Christian Science."

89. Quoted in Massachusetts Citizens for Children, "Federal Legislation Regarding State Religion Exemption Laws." www.masskids.org/dbre/dbre_8.html.

90. Massachusetts Citizens for Children, "Evaluation of Christian Science Claims of Spiritual Healing." www.masskids.org/dbre/dbre_9.html.

91. May, "Challenging Medical Authority."

92. Christian Science, "Christian Science Healing Practices." www.christianscience.com/blogs/articles-journal/christian-science-healing-practices.

93. May, "Challenging Medical Authority."

94. Massachusetts Citizens for Children, "Evaluation of Christian Science Claims of Spiritual Healing."

Chapter 5: The Withdrawal of Life-Sustaining Treatment

95. Burnell, *Final Choices*, p. 107.

96. Paul W. Armstrong and B.D. Cohen, "From Quinlan to Jobes: The Courts and the Persistent Vegetative State Patient," *Hastings Center Report*, February 1, 1988, p. 37.

97. Quoted in Euthanasia—ProCon.org, "In the Absence of an Advance Directive, Who Makes Decisions for Incapacitated Patients?" www.euthanasiaprocon.org/whichfamilymember.html.

98. Colby, *Unplugged*, p. 85.

99. Paul S. Mueller and C. Christopher Hook, "The Terri Schiavo Saga: The Making of a Tragedy and Lessons Learned," *Mayo Clinic Proceedings*, November 1, 2005, p. 1,449. www.mayoclinicproceedings.com/pdf%2F8011%2F8011sa1.pdf.

100. Quoted in Colby, *Unplugged*, p. 126.

101. Burnell, *Final Choices*, p. 74.

102. Quoted in Michael Vitez, "Fighting for the Right to Die," *Philadelphia Inquirer*, May 1, 2006.

103. Quoted in Lief and Caldwell, *And the Walls Came Tumbling Down*, p. 5.

104. Quoted in Lief and Caldwell, *And the Walls Came Tumbling Down*, p. 59.

105. Armstrong and Cohen, "From Quinlan to Jobes."

106. Burnell, *Final Choices*, p. 108.

107. Quoted in National Right to Life, "Terri Schindler-Schiavo —Myths vs. Reality." www.nrlc.org/euthanasia/Terri/mythsv reality.html.

108. Cox, *Hemlock's Cup*, p. 87.

109. Armstrong and Cohen, "From Quinlan to Jobes."

110. Quoted in Meiling Rein, Abbey M. Begun, and Jacquelyn F. Quiram, *Death and Dying: Who Decides?* Wylie, TX: Information Plus, p. 110.

111. David Gibbs and Bob DeMoss, *Fighting for Dear Life*. Minneapolis, MN: Bethany House, 2006, p. 22.

112. National Right to Life, "Terri Schindler-Schiavo—Myths v. Reality."

113. Gibbs and DeMoss, *Fighting for Dear Life*, p. 42.

114. Quoted in Mueller and Hook, "The Terri Schiavo Saga."

115. Quoted in Gibbs and DeMoss, *Fighting for Dear Life*, p. 68.

116. Quoted in United States District Court, Middle District of Florida, Tampa Division, "Case Number 8:05 CV-530-T-27TBM," March 22, 2005. http://fl1.findlaw.com/news.find law.com/hdocs/schiavo/32205fjord.pdf.

117. *Orange County Register*, "Legacy for Life and Death, Schiavo Case Likely to Affect End-of-Life Decisions," April 1, 2005. www.ocregister.com/ocr/sections/news/focus_in_depth/ article_465032.php.

118. Michele Mathes, "Terri Schiavo and End-of-Life Decisions," *Medical-Surgical Nursing*, June 1, 2005, p. 200.

119. Armstrong and Cohen, "From Quinlan to Jobes."

Chapter 1: Death and the Dying Process

1. How has the definition of death changed and why?

2. Explain the importance of Elisabeth Kübler-Ross and her book *On Death and Dying*.

3. In your opinion, what is a "good death"?

Chapter 2: Euthanasia

1. What are the differences between the euthanasia practiced in Nazi Germany and the euthanasia that supporters of the practice propose?

2. Describe the criticism voiced by organized religion to euthanasia.

3. What is the "slippery slope"?

Chapter 3: Assisted Suicide

1. What is assisted suicide?

2. Describe the reasons why people might ask for help in dying.

3. How do the laws regarding assisted suicide in the state of Oregon differ from laws in other states?

Chapter 4: Refusing Medical Treatment

1. Describe the hospice philosophy.

2. How does hospice address the suffering and pain of terminally ill patients?

3. What are some reasons why an individual may refuse medical treatment?

4. Why are medical professionals concerned about religious exemptions to medical care?

Chapter 5: The Withdrawal of Life-Sustaining Treatment

1. What are the characteristics of a persistent vegetative state? How does it differ from a simple coma?

2. What are surrogate decision-makers? What are their responsibilities?

3. Why is there a need for legislation regarding the withdrawal of life-sustaining treatment?

ORGANIZATIONS TO CONTACT

American Hospice Foundation
2120 L St. NW, Ste. 200
Washington, DC 20037
Web site: www.americanhospice.org

A nonprofit organization supporting programs that serve the needs of the terminally ill and grieving. The organization helps train hospice professionals, educates employers about grief issues, and offers in-services at hospices and nursing homes.

Autonomy, Inc.
14 Strawberry Ln.
Danvers, MA 01923
Web site: www.autonomynow.org

This nonprofit organization works with the disabled to make end-of-life decisions. It also works for legislation on end-of-life decisions and choices.

Compassion and Choices
PO Box 101810
Denver, CO 80250-1810
phone: (800) 247-7421
Web site: www.compassionandchoices.org

A nonprofit organization working to improve medical care and expand end-of-life choices. It has sixty chapters throughout the United States. It provides education as well as help with living wills and terminal illness, and it works to help pass legislation dealing with end-of-life decisions.

Death with Dignity National Center
520 SW Sixth Ave., Ste. 1030

Portland, OR 97204
Web site: www.deathwithdignity.org

A nonpartisan, nonprofit organization working for the legal defense and promotion of the Oregon Death with Dignity law. Its purpose is to promote death with dignity initiatives in other parts of the United States.

The Final Exit Network
PO Box 965005
Marietta, GA 30066
Web site: www.finalexitnetwork.org

This organization fosters research into ways to self-deliver, or end one's life. It also promotes the use of advance directives. It advocates for those whose advance directives have not been followed. It is an all-volunteer organization that offers counseling about assisted suicide and other end-of-life decisions.

Human Life Alliance
2855 Anthony Ln. S., Ste. B7
Minneapolis, MN 55418
phone: (651) 484-1040
Web site: www.humanlife.org

This is a nonprofit, pro-life organization that opposes all forms of euthanasia. It works primarily with the disabled and medically vulnerable.

National Hospice and Palliative Care Organization
1700 Diagonal Rd., Ste. 625
Alexandria, VA 22314
Web site: www.nhpco.org

This is a nonprofit organization whose mission is to lead and mobilize social change for improved end-of-life care.

National Right to Life
512 Tenth St. NW
Washington, DC 20004
Web site: www.nrlc.org

This is a nonprofit organization dedicated to pro-life choices. The organization provides information on abortion and euthanasia with an emphasis on restoring legal protection to innocent human life. It offers pro-life resources and also deals with medical ethics.

World Federation of Right to Die Societies
Web site: www.worldrtd.net

This organization is comprised of right-to-die societies from around the world. They hold meetings every two years to discuss end-of-life choices. The member organizations promote voluntary euthanasia and publish information about the right to die. The groups also work for legislation to legalize assisted suicide.

Books

John E. Ferguson, *The Right to Die*. New York: Chelsea House, 2007. A book that examines the right-to-die issue and the history of the movement.

Michael Schiavo with Michael Hirsh, *Terri: The Truth*. New York: Dutton, 2006. A look at Terri Schiavo's illness and death from the viewpoint of her husband, Michael.

Richard Walker, *A Right to Die?* New York: Franklin Watts, 1997. A book that looks at the issue of the right to die.

Mary E. Williams, *Terminal Illness*. San Diego, CA: Greenhaven, 2001. A book that covers the issue of terminal illness and the options available to patients.

Periodicals

Chicago Sun-Times, "Woman Allowed to Die After Six Years in Coma," March 8, 1993. This article describes the battle surrounding Christine Busalacchi, a patient in a persistent vegetative state.

New York Times, "Another Right-to-Die Case Poses New Questions," January 2, 1991. An article that examines two cases involving the withdrawal of life-sustaining treatment.

Liz Townsend, "Kevorkian's Nine-Year Euthanasia Crusade Leads to Murder Conviction," *National Right to Life News*, April 8, 1999. An article detailing Kevorkian's use of his suicide machines, his trial, and his conviction.

Peter A. Ubel, "Assisted Suicide and the Case of Dr. Quill and Diane," *Issues in Law and Medicine*, March 22, 1993. An article describing one of the earliest challenges to assisted suicide laws.

I. Van der Sluis, "The Practice of Euthanasia in the Netherlands," *Issues in Law and Medicine*, March 22, 1989. An article describing the practice of assisted suicide in the Netherlands.

Washington Post, "Congress, the Courts, and the Terri Schiavo Case," March 22, 2005. This article includes readers' opinions about the Schiavo case.

Web Sites

Christian Science Church (www.tfccs.com). A Web site that contains information about the Christian Science Church and its beliefs.

Death with Dignity National Center (www.deathwithdignity .org). A Web site featuring information about the Oregon assisted suicide law.

Euthanasia Research and Guidance Organization (www.final exit.org). This Web site operated by Hemlock Society founder Derek Humphry provides articles and other information about euthanasia.

INDEX

PICTURE CREDITS

Cover photo: Image copyright Claudio Rossol, 2008. Used under license from Shutterstock.com.
Alinari/Art Resource, NY, 11
AP Images, 23, 30, 42, 46, 50, 60, 64, 75, 84
Frank Barratt/Hulton Archive/Getty Images, 67
Giuseppe Cacace/AFP/Getty Images, 87
© Peter Casolino/Alamy, 18
Amy Etra/Time & Life Pictures/Getty Images, 35
Susan M. Gaetz/Getty Images, 51
Getty Images, 92
© Jeff Greenberg/Alamy, 25
John Gress/Getty Images, 54
© Dennis Hallinan/Alamy, 7
© Roberto Herrett/Alamy, 73
Hulton-Deutsch Collection/Corbis, 32
Lee Lockwood/Time & Life Pictures/Getty Images, 57
Arturo Mari/Osservatore Romano/AFP/Getty Images, 38
© Mary Evans Picture Library/Alamy, 13
© Ronnie McMillan/Alamy, 21
Photograph by Dane Penland, Smithsonian Institution. Collection of the Supreme Court of the United States, 59
Keith Philpott/Time & Life Pictures/Getty Images, 88
© PhotoStockFile/Alamy, 96
© Phototake Inc./Alamy, 16, 79, 82
© Ian Shaw/Alamy, 65
© Jack Sullivan/Alamy, 10
© Jim West/Alamy, 39, 71
Steve Zmina, 28, 53

ABOUT THE AUTHOR

Anne Wallace Sharp is the author of the adult book *Gifts*, a compilation of stories about hospice patients; several children's books, including *Daring Pirate Women;* and fifteen other Lucent books. She has also written numerous magazine articles for both adults and juveniles. A retired registered nurse, Sharp has a degree in history. Her interests include reading, traveling, and spending time with her two grandchildren, Jacob and Nicole. Sharp lives in Beavercreek, Ohio.